Plan & Go | Pennine Way

All you need to know to complete Britain's first and finest long-distance trail

Danielle Fenton, Wayne Fenton

sandiburg press

Plan & Go | Pennine Way

All you need to know to complete Britain's first and finest long-distance trail

Copyright © 2016 by Danielle Fenton, Wayne Fenton, and sandiburg press

ISBN 978-1-943126-04-0

Front and back cover photos copyright © 2016 by D. & W. Fenton
Unless otherwise stated, all interior photos by D. & W. Fenton

Published by sandiburg press
www.sandiburgpress.com

Cover photos: High Cup Nick (front); Farmland near Keld (back)

All rights reserved. No part of this publication may be reproduced or transmitted, in any form or by any means, electronically or mechanically, including photo-copying, scanning, recording, or any other information storage and retrieval systems, without written permission of the publisher, except for brief quotations used in reviews.

SAFETY NOTICE: This book describes physically challenging activities in remote outdoor environments which carry an inherent risk of personal injury or death. While the author(s) and sandiburg press have made every effort to ensure that the information contained herein was accurate at the time of publication, they are not liable for any damage, injury, loss, or inconvenience arising directly or indirectly from using this book. Your safety and health during preparations and on the trail are your responsibility. This book does not imply that any of the trails described herein are appropriate for you. Make sure you fully understand the risks, know your own limitations, and always check trail conditions as they can change quickly.

Content

Welcome v
1. Introduction 1
2. **Summary of the Challenge** 5
   a. Requirements 5
   b. Time 6
   c. Budget 9
3. **What to Expect** 13
   a. Trails & Navigation 13
   b. Points of Interest 31
   c. Weather 37
   d. Camping 41
   e. Water 44
   f. Safety 46
   g. Flora & Fauna 50
   h. Other Conditions 53
4. **Long Lead Items** 56
   a. Permits & Regulations 56
   b. Hiking Buddy 58
   c. Travel Arrangements 60
   d. Accommodation 66
5. **Planning & Preparation** 69
   a. Itinerary 69
   b. Food 75
   c. Resupply 78
   d. Training 81

6. Gear 86
   a. Clothing 86
   b. Hiking 89
   c. Sleeping 99
   d. Food & Water 107
   e. Medical & Personal Care 118
   f. Other Essentials 119

7. Personal Experience 122
   a. Plan 122
   b. Go 132

Appendices 164
   A. Checklists 164
   B. Food Suggestions 167
   C. Campsite, Bunkhouse & Hostel Listing 169
   D. Distance Chart 179
   E. Elevation Profiles 180
   F. Links & References 185
   G. List of Abbreviations 187

About the Authors 188

Special Thanks 189

Disclaimer 190

Welcome

This book is a structured guide to support you with any planning and preparation tasks needed to complete England's most famous National Trail, the 268-mile long Pennine Way. Walkers in England long campaigned for the right to roam, so, to many, this cherished national trail is a historical symbol of 'access' to the hills in their beloved country. After celebrating its 50th anniversary as Britain's first ever long-distance path, the Pennine Way certainly comes with a fearsome reputation. After all, you will be taking a journey along the backbone of Britain. Its popularity has never waned, however, and walking the prestigious trail yourself makes you part of its ongoing story.

The challenging nature of the Pennine Way means you should plan ahead and go properly equipped, regardless of whether you intend to tackle the entire route or indeed just one or two sections. Included in this book are itineraries for all walkers. By reading it, you will have a better understanding of the most important hiking information and feel thoroughly prepared to take on this challenge. In addition to providing directions, walking times, and alternative itineraries depending on fitness and experience, we have also included practical information for all budgets based on what to see, where to eat, and, most importantly, where to stay along 'The Way'. The book has been written to save you both time and effort, so that you can put all of your energy into enjoying your trip!

Crossing some of England's grandest and most dramatic landscapes, the route passes through three National Parks, The North Pennines Area of Outstanding Natural Beauty, two National Nature Reserves and 20 Sites of Special Scientific Interest. From the peaty moors of the Peak District in middle England all the way to the quiet, remote Cheviot Hills on the Scottish Borders, the Pennine Way has something to offer every long-distance walker. We hope that our personal experience hiking the trail will inspire you to discover for yourself all of the wonders that are on offer as you prepare to set off on your own Pennine Way adventure.

English Countryside near Cowling, North Yorkshire

1. Introduction

Generally regarded as the toughest, most demanding, and most challenging long-distance walk in Britain, the 268-mile (431km) Pennine Way route was originally the inspiration of walker and writer Tom Stephenson. In an article published in 1935 in the Daily Herald titled 'Wanted: A Long Green Trail', he envisioned a counterpart to America's Appalachian Trail, running through England from the Peak to the Cheviots. That's exactly what transpired when the Pennine Way was designated as Britain's first National Trail by the Countryside Agency in 1965.

What makes the Pennine Way so special is its outstanding natural beauty. It still retains an essence of the wilderness that Tom Stephenson wanted to capture. The main attraction is the wide variety of landscapes the route passes through. Not only will you bear witness to the distinctive charms of three of England's popular national parks – the Peak District, the Yorkshire Dales, and the Northumberland National Park – but also quickly discover that along the entire trail there are many significant historical and cultural points of interest, too.

Edale in the Peak District is the official start point of the Pennine Way, with the preferred direction of travel going south to north. The official end point is Kirk Yetholm, a small village just over the Scottish border, which you will reach after traversing the Cheviot Hills. Completing the full distance is a demanding undertaking that requires thorough preparation and a basic understanding of hill walking and navigation. However, there is nothing technically difficult about the trail.

If you complete the entire trail, a free celebratory drink awaits you at the Border Hotel in Kirk Yetholm, as was the custom started by Alfred Wainwright in 1968 when he offered to buy a half-pint of beer for anyone who managed to walk the 268-mile route. But what he considered a 'tiresome trudge' has by no means put off thousands of thru-hikers from completing Britain's first national trail. Wainwright's generosity has been estimated to have cost him up to £15,000 by his death in 1991!

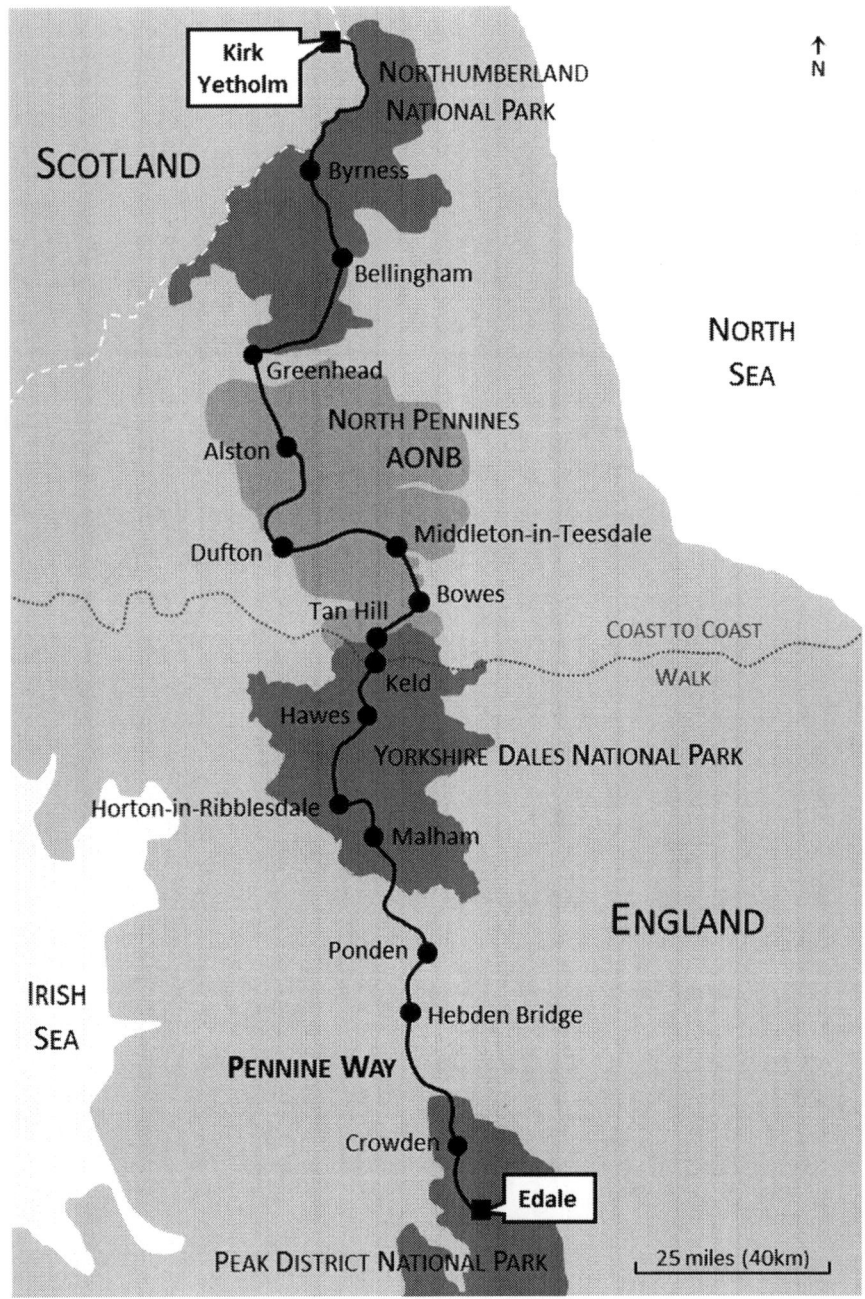

Figure 1 – Overview Map of the Pennine Way

If you make it all the way to the sleepy Scottish village of Kirk Yetholm, then fittingly, The Border Hotel – recognised as the official end-point of the Pennine Way – still honours this tradition. Alongside your beer, further recognition of your achievement is the award of a Pennine Way certificate of completion, a touching keepsake at the end of your journey.

So what prompted us to take on the challenge of the Pennine Way? We've always had a passion for travel and after taking a career break a few years ago to set off on our own adventure to see 'the world', we saw ourselves developing a love of walking. Having completed several shorter hiking trails around the world, it made it ever more apparent to us how little we knew of hiking in our home country. England certainly has much to offer in terms of 'the great outdoors', so it was time for us to take advantage of the beautiful areas of mountains, meadows, moorlands, woods, wetlands, and ultimately the wonderful walking trails that are practically on our doorstep. It was time for us to set off on our first long-distance hike in England and see whether Tom Stephenson's legacy fulfilled his vision.

The 268-mile walk, which we had been planning for over a year, was a personal challenge, a means of training for a further long-distance hike that we had planned in the USA, and a fundraising event. But more than that, hiking the Pennine Way allowed us to visit places in England we had never been to before, which we were quick to discover can boast such outstanding natural beauty they can seriously rival anywhere else in the world! If you are reading this book, then we know you are also convinced of this and the value of attempting Britain's first long-distance path.

With this book, we provide a clear picture of what you should expect on the Pennine Way and how best to prepare yourself. Chapter 2 describes the physical challenges of the route and gives guidance on estimating the time and budget you will need to complete it. Chapter 3 lets you know what to expect regarding weather and trail conditions. It also covers camping, access to food and water supplies along the way, and recommendations for your personal safety. The initial estimate of your trail hiking days allows you to prepare the Long Lead items of Chapter 4, such as travel plans and transportation links for getting to and from the start and end points. How to prepare for all this physically and logistically is the topic of Chapter 5. Chapter 6 then takes a closer look at gear options more suitable for the Pennines and offers advice on their correct use. Finally, Chapter 7 offers some personal experiences and anecdotes from our own Pennine Way adventure.

We hope you will find all the information you need to make your hike an enjoyable and memorable experience for all the right reasons.

Let the Pennine Way enrich your life. Happy hiking!

Visit *www.PlanAndGoHiking.com* for more information and pictures.

2. Summary of the Challenge

Can you walk the Pennine Way? If you are interested in hiking and have some experience, the answer is most definitely YES! This long-distance trail will not be without its challenges, however. The presence of some steep gradients and troublesome moorland terrain coupled with the inclement weather that England is so famous for can be enough to test the resolve of the most hardened hiker. That being said, thousands of people undertake the walk each year. The vast majority of these people do not go walking every weekend or indeed every month. However, they have all increased their level of fitness and stamina before embarking on this journey. By and large, if you have done your research and are thoroughly prepared, then the Pennine Way is achievable with a good set of 'walking legs' and sheer determination.

a. Requirements

Completing the full distance is a demanding undertaking that requires preparation and some understanding of hill walking and navigation. If you are averagely fit, have no health issues, and are carrying no injuries, then you will be in good shape to attempt this long-distance hike. There is nothing technically difficult about the Pennine Way. You won't find yourself dangling off ropes, clinging to rock faces, or staring down into a terrifying abyss. Your main adversaries are the varying terrain, England's temperate maritime climate, and the overwhelming sense of aloneness you feel as the route takes you through the quieter, more remote parts of the country the further north you go.

Apart from summiting Pen-y-Ghent in the Yorkshire Dales at 694 metres (2,277 ft.), you will find the North Pennines to have the steepest climbs of the entire trip. Here, you will face the highest point of the trail, which is Cross Fell at 893 metres (2,930 ft.). No matter your itinerary or preference of walking direction, you will generally find this to be in the middle of your trip, so you should be well acclimatised for the elevation gains, particularly as most people see an improvement in their overall fitness and stamina after their first few days of walking.

In addition to a good level of fitness and endurance, you will need a strong back and knees to carry a full backpack (approx. 12-20kg/25-45 lbs.) if you plan to bring your own camping gear. It really helps if you can share the load with a hiking buddy in terms of tent, cooking equipment, and food supplies. If you intend to camp along the route, you must be able to set up your own tent, use a gas stove, and deal with nature's call in the wild.

Despite the Pennine Way taking you to some of the remoter parts of the country, it is not a typical wilderness trail. Apart from the very last stages of the walk, where you will head into the Cheviot Hills straddling the Anglo-Scottish border, you are never far from civilisation. If you plan your days carefully and make your miles, you should arrive at an established campsite along the path. In the remoter regions, you have the option to take refuge in a mountain hut. Alternatively, if you wish to enjoy a few more home comforts after a long day of walking, accommodation options to suit all budgets are plentiful along most of the route.

b. Time

The best time to set out on the Pennine Way is during the summer months (June-August), but hardy, experienced hikers may attempt it all year round. Most people complete the trail successfully in 14-24 days. The actual time will vary dependent upon your age, level of fitness, and overall schedule. The purest way is to carry everything with you and camp. It takes longer because you are carrying more weight and therefore covering less distance each day. An average fit walker should complete the walk in about 21 days, which approximates to 12-13 miles per day. In order to fully appreciate all that the Pennine Way has to offer, an itinerary of 21 days is perfect, as this will enable you to complete the route within a 3-week leave.

ⓘ *Trivia fact:* Nine people have completed the Pennine Way in under three days from start to finish, which involves virtually continuous running with possibly less than three hours of sleep in those 72 hours.

However, the fastest time to date was recorded on 23rd July 1989. English fell-runner Mike Hartley ran the entire route, finishing in just 2 days, 17 hours, 20 minutes, and 15 seconds! To achieve this record time, Hartley did two years of research on the Pennine Way and peaked his training at 170 miles per week. Impressively, he ran without stopping for sleep. In fact, he stopped only twice for 18 minutes each time, once for fish and chips in Alston! The Pennine Way did, however, take its toll on his feet. He ran the last 40 miles with a borrowed size 10 shoe on his ordinarily size 8 right foot.

But what time is right for you? In order to have an adequate challenge, start by planning your days on the trail. Whilst you are doing this, remember why you are attempting this hike in the first place. Is it to gain that sense of achievement once completed? Is it to simply enjoy the breathtaking scenery along the way? The Pennine Way will certainly provide you with both. The key to both enjoyment and satisfaction though is not pushing yourself too hard.

Figure 2 is intended to provide guidance for an initial assessment. Selecting your age and corresponding fitness level will give you an idea of how many days you will take for hiking the backbone of England. For example, a 40-year-old person of average fitness should plan to take roughly 18-20 days, so let's say 19.

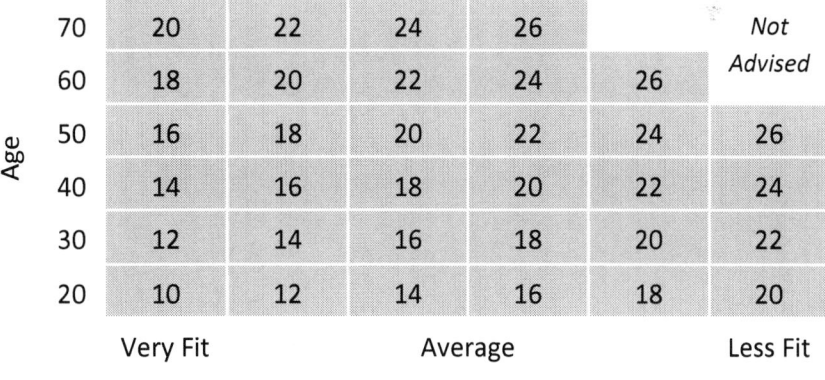

Figure 2 – Estimate of Trail Days on the Pennine Way

Summary of the Challenge

With your estimate of trail days (ETD), you can calculate your average miles per day by dividing the total distance by your ETD:

Average miles per day = 268 miles / ETD

Taking the above example leads to an average of 268/19 = 14 miles per day. While this is a good initial estimate, additional factors need to be taken into consideration as they may affect your total ETD. Schedules can vary greatly on how one allocates time on and off the trail, both for hiking and relaxing. In order to account for these differences and to give you a more personalised hiking itinerary, consider the following questions:

Would you like to do any side trips or take rest days to relax?

- If yes, add one day to your ETD for every side trip and/or rest day.

Would you like to take extra time along the trail to stop at rivers, meadows, etc. for bird watching, photography, relaxing, or other?

- If yes, add the multiple of half/full days you would like to take as extra time to your ETD.

Would you like to include extra time for poor weather conditions?

- If yes, add the multiple of half/full days you would like to include as cushion to your ETD.

With your initial ETD from Figure 2 and the additional days resulting from above questions, calculate your total days on the trail. In our example, the 40-year-old hiker chooses to add three days to the initial ETD: two days for side trips and resting plus one day for possible bad weather. Stops at villages and landmarks along with photography will be integrated with food breaks to not consume additional time. This leads to a total estimate of 22 days.

The resulting total ETD should be the basis for all your subsequent planning regarding travel, food, and resupply. If you cannot answer the above questions just yet, don't worry. You may only know whether or not you would like to go on side trips after you learn more about available options in the next chapter. Any extra days may also be dependent on the quality of the weather, but you will at least be aware of the possibilities. This could be allowing for extra days in the Yorkshire Dales, where the scenery is spectacular, or lingering longer in the Cheviots, where it is very remote and you can feel the isolation that is rarely encountered in the UK.

Whilst planning and preparing for our own Pennine Way journey, we had allowed ourselves a generous and leisurely 25-day itinerary to take account of several side trips we had planned, with the possibility of some zero hiking days if needed. In comparison, we met a few very fit hikers who planned on completing the entire trail in 14 days, whereas others had a 21-day itinerary, which is a much more reasonable pace for this walk.

(i) If you can afford the time, we recommend taking a slower pace to allow yourself the opportunity to really appreciate the contrasting English landscape and the variation of communities generally reflected in the architecture, customs, and dialect that will greet you on your journey north.

As an alternative to walking the Pennine Way in its entirety, you could decide to break it up into stages and hike a section at a time over a longer period. In Section 3a *Trails & Navigation*, we have picked out for you and highlighted six of the most iconic sections of the route that will give you a good taste of the adventure at hand. Once you progress onto more challenging fell walks or scrambles, you can reach a real sense of achievement and exhilaration and will no doubt be ready to tackle the full 268 miles.

c. Budget

How and when you decide to tackle the walk will determine what you will ultimately spend on the Pennine Way. There are generally three budget options linked to where you choose to sleep and how you get your meals, which could be from a pub/restaurant or cooked at camp if you are trying to minimise your spending.

The most expensive option would be to hike the Pennine Way by a series of day walks between hotels or B&Bs, where you would sleep each evening and eat meals prepared by the establishment. With this option, you could also utilise a logistical service company and have your luggage transferred between destinations. Although this would be an additional expense, it means you can carry a lighter daypack that has just your essentials in it, which makes for less demanding walking days.

Eating out along the way is the most expensive food option on the trail. Hotels, B&Bs, and local pubs normally provide meals, but this will cost you significantly more money than if you cooked your own. On the Pennine Way, it is more commonplace along the route to find B&Bs, which are generally less expensive than hotels. When working out your budget, it is worth remembering that if you choose to stay in accommodation along the way, breakfasts are usually included in the price of an evening stay, so that is one meal per day already taken care of.

Hostels are a good budget option if you prefer to hike without a tent and need overnight accommodation. You can maximise your spending here by sharing the cost with a hiking buddy or several others by choosing to sleep in a shared room. Many hostels also provide camping as well as cooking areas that can be used by guests, thereby helping you to reduce food costs if you are not eating out. Sometimes cooking equipment and utensils are provided for your use, meaning you could buy your food locally at a shop and cook it yourself. This helps if you do not want to carry the extra weight of cooking gear and choose to do a mixture of eating out and cooking your own meals.

The cheapest and most favourable option on the Pennine Way is to go traditional and walk the route with a full backpack, camping along the way. Carrying all your own gear (tent, stove, sleeping gear, etc.) means that you will be self-sufficient and can minimise both accommodation and food costs. Campsite fees are much cheaper than the nightly rates at a hotel or B&B, and despite the fact that the cost of food is incredibly variable, cooking your own will help to keep your budget in check.

Bear in mind, camping is the most cost-effective choice and lowest budget option assuming you already own the equipment needed to sleep comfortably in your tent. However, if you have to buy much of the necessary gear, then this will significantly increase your expenses. Even though purchasing brand new gear may put a hefty dent in your budget, investing in thoroughly researched gear is definitely worth your time and money. Your gear is your life on the trail, but it is also worth remembering that more expensive does not always translate to better!

The middle cost option would be to stay in a bunkhouse or camping barn along the route, providing you with a bed (or bunk) each evening. This would also enable you to hike without the need for a tent, thereby reducing the weight of your pack. However, you are usually required to provide your own sleeping bag and may need a basic liner depending on what the establishment provides as standard.

The season in which you intend to walk the Pennine Way will also have an impact on the overall budget needed. If you choose to hike in the summer months of June, July, or August, you will find this to be the most expensive time of the year, as these are considered to be the best months in terms of English weather. Likewise, if your walk coincides with a school or public holiday, this will also affect your booking options.

Generally, camping spots can be found at most times of the year, as a backpacking tent takes up very little space. If you are trying to maximise your budget and keep costs low, then setting off in the spring or autumn can mean both significant savings and greater availability of accommodation options. Hiking during the off-season can be at the risk of more unstable and unsuitable weather, but as the English climate is so unpredictable anyway, it might be worth the risk. A little flexibility in your itinerary may work out very beneficial for your budget!

The final expense that has to be considered quite early is the cost of your transport to and from the trail. If you live in the UK, then this will not be as significant in comparison to a walker who has to travel from overseas. In general, England is not a cheap place to go travelling. You may find yourself adding on lots of little extras – fish and chips or an ice-cream here and there, souvenirs, internet use, laundry. A good idea is to allow yourself a 'slush fund' for any rainy day expenses. This could be opting to stay in a hostel due to bad weather or simply allowing yourself a couple of extra pints at the end of a particularly tough day. As you pass through so many delightful villages on the Pennine Way south and central sections, it would be a shame not sample their hospitality from time to time.

Table 1 below lists some sample costs to give an indication of possible daily budgets. Actual costs could differ significantly as these are very subjective to personal preference and taste. (Cost of drinks generally allows for two purchases.) You may find that mixing between the options may offer some savings along the way.

	High		Medium		Low	
Accommodation	Hotel	£100	B&B	£60	Campsite	£6
Breakfast	Included	-	Included	-	Home-cooked	£2.50
Lunch	Packed Lunch	£6	Packed Lunch	£6	Local Shop	£3.50
Dinner	Restaurant	£20	Pub	£13	Home-Cooked	£5
Snacks	Local Shop	£2	Local Shop	£2	Local Shop	£2
Drink	Bar	£10	Pub	£7	Cafe	£5
		£138		**£88**		**£24**

Table 1 – Estimate of Daily Costs (Single Occupancy) by Budget Option

Summary of the Challenge

3. What to Expect

This chapter is intended to give you an impression of the highlights and unique conditions along the Pennine Way. The changeable weather will most likely affect your choice of equipment the most, so the following sections will help guide you in choosing your gear and making other preparations for the hike. Later in the book, you can compare your thoughts with a gear overview in Chapter 6 and our personal experiences in Chapter 7.

a. Trails & Navigation

The National Trails website, which might be considered authoritative, gives the length of the Pennine Way as 268 miles, while the Pennine Way Association give it as 256 miles. On the OS 1:25,000 Explorer map, the official Pennines Way route measures 244 miles long. The reality is that because of the many optional variations, temporary diversions, and your own deviations for refreshments or accommodation, the actual mileage for any individual will probably be somewhere between the two extremes of 244 and 268 miles, or perhaps even more.

Trailheads & Walking Direction

Edale in the Peak District has always been considered the official start point of the Pennine Way, with the preferred direction of travel going south to north. This is for no other reason than it being the direction in which most guidebooks are written, so you may in fact want to throw caution to the wind and walk the route in the opposite direction. From Edale, you will take Jacob's Ladder to cross the gritstone moors of the Peak District National Park into the Calder Valley, where the Industrial Revolution was born. You will then traverse the windswept moors of Bronte country past 'Top Withens', said to be the inspiration for the house in Emily Bronte's novel, Wuthering Heights. Meandering through rolling farmland into the stunning Yorkshire Dales, the route then takes in the striking limestone cliffs of Malham as well as taking you to the summit of Pen-y-Ghent, the shapeliest of the Yorkshire 'Three Peaks', before continuing on into beautiful Swaledale.

You'll be ready for a pit-stop as the Pennine Way then climbs up to Tan Hill and the isolated 17th century inn that stands atop it, maintaining its record as the highest pub in England situated at 528 metres (1,732 ft.). After following the River Tees, and crossing the wild, empty moors of the North Pennines, next you will visit the charming English village of Dufton with its traditional, cosy inn, before ascending Cross Fell, the highest point of the Pennine Way at 893 metres (2,930 ft.). From here, you may experience breathtaking views across to the Lakeland fells in the west of England if the weather is clear.

The route then heads east where you will walk some historic milestones next to the best-preserved section of Hadrian's Wall. After marvelling at such archaeological riches left behind by the Romans, the Pennine Way heads north again at Housesteads Fort – the most complete Roman fort in Britain, weaving its way through vast woodland to the tiny hamlet of Byrness. Now, in the remotest region that the Pennine Way crosses, you will experience real isolation whilst traversing the Cheviot Hills before reaching the end-point of the trail just over the Scottish border, in the small village of Kirk Yetholm.

Trail Conditions & Route

At least half of the route meanders over open moorland or through pastures, only a tenth is forest, woodland, or river bank. But don't be lulled into a false sense of security thinking this will be an easy countryside stroll, as a walker completing the full route will climb a total of 12,000 metres! Relative to other British long-distance walks, the Pennine Way retains its fearsome reputation as the toughest. Despite this, it remains a popular choice with about 15,000 long-distance walkers and more than 250,000 day walkers using all or part of the trail each year, contributing millions of pounds to the local economy and hundreds of jobs along the way. The route also forms part of a European long-distance path called the E2.

The terrain on the Pennine Way is varied. In some places, such as Malham Cove and High Force, the paths are smooth and firm, but in others the path may be narrow and uneven or wet and boggy. During the 1970s and 80s, erosion caused by constant foot traffic meant that walkers on the Pennine Way frequently had to wade through deep bogs. Since then, conditions along the path have improved significantly. Stone slabs have been laid on the worst affected areas to minimalise trail erosion, with several sections of the trail being completely rebuilt.

As the Pennines get more than their fair share of rain, much of the length of the trail is persistently wet so you should still be prepared for traversing wet peat bogs on at least a few days. Regular work is now necessary to keep the Pennine Way accessible, hence improvements are always ongoing. But the benefits are such that the trail is much less forbidding than what some walkers have experienced in the past. If the weather has been kind then you may well get away with dry socks, but it wouldn't be the Pennine Way if bog was no longer a hazard.

Keep in mind you will be following a mountain range. The Pennines is both hilly and remote in places but most ascents on the route are gentle gradients up grassy moorland. However, in a small number of places the trail does take you up steeper ground. For example, the ascent of Pen-y-Ghent involves two short but steep rocky sections and the route to Cauldron Snout crosses two short boulder fields beside the River Tees, then climbs steeply up the rocks beside the waterfall. For regular walkers these sections shouldn't be a problem, but for those that are less experienced know your limitations.

In contrast to Scotland's long-distance footpath – the West Highland Way, which is a week-long trek from Glasgow to Fort William, the Pennine Way has slightly longer distances between accommodation, more climbing and more walking on high, exposed ground. But the biggest difference is probably the Pennine Way's rough and sometimes wet ground, in place of the West Highland Way's solid tracks.

What to Expect

Compared to the Coast to Coast, which is the fortnight-long path across England from St Bees on the Irish Sea coast in the west to Robin Hood's Bay on the North Sea coast in the east, the Pennine Way is very similar in some respects. The Lake District stages on the Coast to Coast for example are sharper and steeper but the Pennine stages are comparable in elevation gain.

Overall, having experienced all three long-distance walks, we found that the Pennine Way spends more time on high, wild ground, and is tougher and more remote than either of the previous two. Be prepared to face some long, arduous days, where it will be a challenge to continue, particularly when your legs are fatigued and you are faced with biting cold winds and driving rain. However, don't let that put you off. Each day of walking will be varied and every day on the route is a real treasure.

Pennine Way South – Edale to Horton-in-Ribblesdale

The Pennine Way officially starts in the Peak District National Park at the village of Edale, right outside the 16th century Old Nags Head pub, where it is customary to enjoy a drink in the Hiker Bar before setting off. The path then reaches Kinder Downfall by skirting the southern edge of the Kinder plateau to ascend Jacob's Ladder, an ancient packhorse route at the head of the Edale Valley, leading you to Kinder Low and along the western edge of the gritstone plateau to reach the Downfall.

After reaching Kinder Downfall, the route heads north-west along the edge of the plateau before descending to Ashop Head, then climbing up to Mill Hill to follow the long ridge which connects Kinder to Bleaklow. The traverse of the Dark Peak – the peat moorlands of Kinder Scout, Bleaklow and Black Hill can be considered a tough section to be faced with after almost immediately commencing your Pennine Way journey. Here, the terrain can still be very boggy. Slabs, introduced by the authorities to minimise erosion caused by decades of walkers, make this once problematic section of the walk much more enjoyable and now lead the way over Mill Hill, over Featherbed Moss, and onto Bleaklow.

Next, the Pennine Way path crosses the Snake Road, which is the A57 linking Manchester with Sheffield, and the old track known as Doctor's Gate, then follows a feature known as Devil's Dike to reach Hern Clough, the upper section of the Alport river. This is followed upstream to the Wain Stones and Bleaklow Head, the high point of this hill. At a height of 633 metres, Bleaklow famously contains the wreckage of an old US Air Force bomber that crashed on the hillside in 1948, killing all 13 crew members. The site is so well known that Pennine Way walkers regularly divert off route to pay their respects.

Sitting a short way from Bleaklow's summit, the Wain Stones are a pair of weathered stones which, from the right angle, give the impression of an old man and woman puckering up for a kiss. It's a famous photo opportunity with walkers who strive to get the shot and angle just right!

From Bleaklow the path swings west for a short distance to drop into the stream system of Torside Clough, which descends to Crowden in the Longendale valley. From Crowden the path follows the west bank of Great Crowden Brook upstream to Black Hill, detouring at Oaken Clough to climb over the top of Laddow Rocks. At the head of the clough, the route heads straight up Dun Hill to reach the summit of Black Hill, an extremely boggy area known as Soldier's Lump.

Here, the path divides, with the modern advised route heading almost north to drop down to Wessenden Head, which then follows the chain of Wessenden Reservoirs down to Marsden. The original Pennine Way route continuing north-west has been abandoned due to the severe erosion caused by thousands of pairs of walking boots.

North of the Dark Peak, you come to waterworks country and progress is fast on rough tracks beside silent, brooding reservoirs, with impressive views of Greater Manchester and much of Lancashire to your left. Magnificent in their bleakness, these are the Pennine moors, where Derbyshire, Cheshire, Lancashire and West Yorkshire meet. Navigation is potentially tricky only along Blackstone Edge in foul weather, but there are cairns and poles to guide you.

The next civilisation you reach is the town of Hebden Bridge nestling below the monument on Stoodley Pike, which seems to be visible from all over the Calder Valley. Take time to enjoy the wooded river valleys hereabouts, before climbing out over the Haworth moors, the so-called Bronte country. Top Withens, a ruined farmhouse said to have been the inspiration for the Earnshaw family house in Emily Brontë's *Wuthering Heights* is visited next as the Pennine Way progresses north. Again, route finding could be testing over Heptonstall Moor and Ickornshaw Moor in unfriendly conditions. Likewise, the twists and turns climbing up the Calder Valley need close attention.

Ahead of you now is the county of North Yorkshire and the gentler farming country of the Aire Gap. 'Mostly muck and manure' is how the ever-joyful Alfred Wainwright described the first part of this section. The Aire Gap are the lowlands, which form a geographical corridor between the South Pennines and the Yorkshire Dales, or between millstone grit moors and limestone. The Romans built a road through it, but Bronze Age traders had long since used the route to travel between Ireland and Scandinavia.

There are fine 360-degree views of North Yorkshire's countryside from the vantage point of Pinhaw Beacon, where beyond lies the picturesque village of Thornton in Craven. Similarly, the bench atop Scaleber Hill is a good place to take a rest break and soak up the scenery before heading into the charming village of Gargrave. Rolling pastures and flowering meadows give way to flat riverside walking where barge and bridge enthusiasts will enjoy strolling along the Leeds to Liverpool canal taking their time to admire the collection of narrow boats moored at East Marton.

Leaving Gargrave, the Pennine Way follows the River Aire, after which you will cross into the Yorkshire Dales National Park and enter the remarkable limestone scenery of Malhamdale. The domain of extreme rock climbers and peregrine falcons. The magnificent limestone cliffs of Malham Cove are one of the highlights of the route, famously appearing in both *Harry Potter and the Deathly Hallows* and the Steve Coogan series *The Trip*.

From Malham to Horton-in-Ribblesdale, the next highlights of the Pennine Way are the major hills of Fountains Fell and Pen-y-Ghent, one of the well-known *Yorkshire Three Peaks*. At 668 metres (2,191 ft.), the trail first crosses Fountains Fell about a third of a mile north of the summit. For the northbound walker, this is approximately 85 miles (137km) from the start of the Pennine Way at Edale and is the first point where the trail climbs higher than Kinder Scout's 636 metres (2,087 ft.), which was reached soon after the start.

Pen-y-Ghent

The route then continues down the western slopes of the fell and ascends the southern ridge of Pen-y-Ghent. This summit of 694 metres (2,277 ft.) now supplants Fountains Fell as the highest point yet reached on the Pennine Way. Route Finding is straightforward, though you wouldn't want to be caught out on Pen-y-Ghent in rough weather. From here, it is a relatively easy downhill walk to the village of Horton-in-Ribblesdale, where an overnight stop and a well-deserved rest beckons.

Pennine Way Central – Horton-in-Ribblesdale to Greenhead

Horton-in-Ribblesdale can be considered a milestone in your epic journey north, as from here you will start the Pennine Way Central Section. From Horton to the busy market town of Hawes, it is a simple, but lonely and somewhat exposed trek among moorland pastures close to the main watershed of Britain. Up there, in the vague country between the upper reaches of Ribblesdale, Wharfedale, and Wensleydale, the land is empty but the views are impressive. The topography is one of broad, flat moorland ridges and the predominant rock is limestone once again, which gives so much of the central Dales their unique flavour.

Between Horton and Hawes, the Pennine Way makes use of a network of old drove roads, of which at least one is Roman in origin. After crossing Ling

What to Expect

Gill by an ancient packhorse bridge, the trail rises to the watershed once more at Cam End.

This was an important road junction in ancient times and nowadays is just as important to the long-distance path network, for this is where the Pennine Way joins the Dales Way. The combined Pennine Way and Dales Way head northwestwards along Cam High Road. Cam High Road is an old Roman road and, in common with most of the roads constructed in that era, is as straight as an arrow. The Dales Way drops to the right into the Oughtershaw valley and ultimately into upper Wharfedale, whereas the Pennine Way heads onwards along the top of a windy moorland ridge, eventually reaching the limit of a tarmac road at Kidhow Gate.

From Kidhow Gate, the Pennine Way leaves the Roman road and instead runs along West Cam Road, along the western slopes of Dodd Fell. The picturesque valley of Snaizeholme Beck lies down to the west. After what seems like walking several miles with stone underfoot, the path drops down the long northern spine of Dodd Fell and veers northeast, into the delightful stone built village of Gayle. A simple flagged path leads the short distance into the friendly town of Hawes, home of the Wensleydale cheese factory – a recommended side trip if time allows.

Beyond Hawes, the great bulwark of Great Shunner Fell is what you will face next on your Pennine Way journey. At 716 metres (2349 ft.), it is the third highest mountain in the Yorkshire Dales. Take relief in the fact that there isn't a steep climb up. Due to its popularity with day walkers, efforts have been made to alleviate the erosion caused by so much foot traffic with the construction of a flagstone path, which now provides a clear and direct route to the summit.

After crossing the summit of Great Shunner Fell, the Pennine Way leads you into glorious, green Swaledale. Now in quintessential Dales farmland where fields are lined with dry stone walls, look out for any traditional two-level barns. The design is rarely seen elsewhere and there are literally hundreds of such barns dotted around the Dales providing a unique photo opportunity. Usually built away from the main farm buildings, the barns were designed in such a way that the animals could be housed inside on the ground floor, whilst the feed was kept safely on the first level.

It is a picturesque walk from the charming village of Thwaite, around the eastern flanks of Kisdon Hill to the village of Keld. A stony path heads east up steep slopes clad in bracken and heather. Make sure you pause to look back at Great Shunner Fell which dominates the view along with Lovely Seat – the highest summit on the eastern side of the Buttertubs Pass separating Wensleydale and Swaledale. The route then joins a grassy track at Kisdon House farm, where you continue heading up beside a lime kiln.

The route follows a path contouring around the side of the hill, picking its way awkwardly through belts of slippery scree. To the right are stunning views over the deep valley of the River Swale – the 'swirling river' – the dramatic scenery of Upper Swaledale fashioned during the last Ice Age. Here, you can see the gorge of Swinner Gill cutting down through the scarp of Ivelet Moor. The path then runs above steep, wooded slopes, eventually passing through an overgrown quarry. When the path turns down towards a footbridge you are only minutes away from the village of Keld, which is a prominent overnight stop with long-distance hikers, as it is where the Pennine Way and the Coast to Coast path meet.

From Keld, the Pennine Way winds northwards to Tan Hill, where it is customary to have a drink, whether it be a pot of tea or a pint of ale, at Britain's highest pub – the Tan Hill Inn – which dates back to the 17th century. Standing at 528 metres (1732 ft.), it is situated on the borders of Yorkshire, Cumbria, and Durham. At this point, you might find it heartening to know that you have actually reached what is considered to be the halfway point of the Pennine Way!

After a well-deserved rest at the Tan Hill Inn, the route crosses Sleightholme Moor to the Stainmore Gap. The picturesque views of unceasing stretches of peat and purple heather should help to take your mind off the fact you will most likely be trudging over endless, often squelchy moorland. From our own experience, we found this to be one of the worst sections of the Pennine Way for bog, resulting in unavoidable soggy feet, before the traditional Dales town of Middleton-in-Teesdale is reached.

Once the archetypal 'company town', owned lock, stock, and barrel by the Quaker-run London Lead Company, Teesdale is now the gateway to arguably one of the finest stretches of the Pennine Way. The route follows the River Tees upstream to the village of Dufton in the Eden Valley, known as 'the valley of the ice flowers'. Have your camera ready as you pass through species-rich upland hay meadows bursting with wildflowers and walk alongside the impressive waterfalls of High Force, Low Force, and Cauldron Snout below the dam of Cow Green Reservoir. You will then reach one of the Pennine Way's best landmarks – the spectacular glaciated U-shaped chasm of High Cup Nick on the western flanks of the North Pennines Area of Outstanding Natural Beauty (AONB).

Low Force

Taking the Narrow Gate path down the right-hand side of the Cup, make sure you stop to look back up the valley as it is the best way to admire the cliffs. The track then meets a wall which is your first chance of shelter in inclement weather, then joins onto an old drove road. Walking on the western side of the Pennines for the first time, it is a gradual descent to the pretty village of Dufton. The village has old and new houses arranged around a small green, with the main facilities needed by every walker – a campsite, youth hostel, shop, and most importantly a pub!

From Dufton, the Pennine Way climbs back up the fells, passing in turn the summits of Knock Fell, Great Dun Fell, Little Dun Fell, and finally Cross Fell, at 893 metres (2,930 ft.), the highest point on the entire trail. This section is considered demanding, and most walkers have a long day ahead facing the 21-mile traverse of Cross Fell and its satellites. Here, walkers can face tricky conditions in bad weather as a result of the Helm Wind which sweeps down the south-west slope of the escarpment.

This lengthy stage from Dufton to Garrigill can be broken up by making use of the bothy, Greg's Hut, which is situated at a strategic place on the Pennine Way, just to the north of the summit of Cross Fell. The hut originally served as a shop where miners stayed during the working week and has subsequently been restored by the Mountain Bothies Association to provide shelter for walkers caught out in bad weather. Be prepared for the long descent that follows to the valley of the South Tyne at Garrigill. The trail then keeps close to the river to reach the town of Alston. With a wide range of amenities, Alston is an excellent overnight stop if you have walked this far and are in need of some respite.

From Alston, the route then continues down the valley of the South Tyne to Slaggyford and Knarsdale. Above the village of Lambley the trail leaves the valley to cross more moorland to the A69 near the village of Greenhead. Outside Greenhead, the Pennine Way passes Thirlwall Castle on Hadrian's Wall – the 2000-year-old frontier of the former Roman empire. It is a popular stage with section hikers and is another Pennine Way classic. Part of the movie *Robin Hood: Prince of Thieves* was filmed at Sycamore Gap on Hadrian's Wall. It is worth noting that this section gets very busy at times, as the *Hadrian's Wall Path* is an 84-mile long-distance trail in its own right.

Pennine Way North – Greenhead to Kirk Yetholm

For the next 11 miles (18km) or so, the Pennine Way coincides with the Hadrian's Wall Path, following the wall closely past Once Brewed to Rapishaw Gap, a mile west of the Housesteads Roman Fort. Considered the most dramatic stretch of the wall, marvel at the defensive construction before the trail finally leaves the Pennine hills behind and strikes out across Northumberland National Park to Bellingham on the North Tyne.

From the wall, the route to the large village of Bellingham heads north through Wark Forest, (which is the southern part of Kielder Forest), then follows field paths to Shitlington Crags. More remote country follows, across Padon Hill and the edge of Redesdale Forest. The trail eventually reaches Redesdale at Blakehopeburnhaugh and Cottonshope-burnfoot, two neighbouring hamlets, which compete for the longest name in England. It is an isolated day of walking across lonely moors following the River Rede upstream, which eventually brings you to the village of Byrness.

Byrness is your last resupply point, as the final 25 miles of the Pennine Way (27 miles if you choose the side trip to the Cheviot summit) lies along the spine of the Cheviot Hills, which mark the border between England and Scotland, and there is no habitation. You must either come off the ridge at the Border Gate (approximately 14 miles from Byrness) and walk around two and a half miles to Cocklawfoot farm on the Scottish side. There is a public road that allows walkers to temporarily exit the trail and take pre-arranged transportation to their choice of overnight lodging, returning to the trailhead the following morning to continue on to Kirk Yetholm. Or, you must carry a tent and wild camp at Davidson's Linn, a remote waterfall that takes you to within a kilometre of the Anglo-Scottish Border.

On this last section, there are also two mountain refuge huts or bothies, where you can seek shelter in an emergency. Therefore, another possibility to break up the last 25 miles could be to make use of the Auchope Refuge, which is the closest mountain hut to Kirk Yetholm, and sleep rough if you arrive late and leave early. The only other option is to attempt to walk the whole 25 miles in one day, an arduous journey which is likely to take anywhere between 12-15 hours.

From Byrness, the trail climbs steeply from the village, then heads north to cross the Scottish border near Ogre Hill. For the rest of this final stage, the path switches back and forth between England and Scotland, along a fence which marks the border itself. Back in England, the trail passes the Roman fort at Chew Green and briefly follows the Roman road of Dere Street, both sites of archaeological importance. After 9 miles or so, it may be prudent to take a rest break and eat lunch at the first mountain refuge hut known as 'Yearning Saddle', located on Lamb Hill. The basic wooden shelter also offers respite from persistent wind on the walk. The path then follows the Border Ridge, passing the King's Seat and the high point of Windy Gyle at 619m (2030 ft.), where, true to its name, you can literally be blown off your feet in the raging winds and changing weather conditions.

Cheviot Summit Junction

On reaching the 743-metre (2,438 ft.) top of Cairn Hill, there is a path junction where you can take a side trip to the summit of the Cheviot, the highest summit in the Cheviot Hills at 815 metres (2,674 ft.). It is the last major peak on the Pennine Way in the far north of England. It is a two-mile out-and-back side trip to the Cheviot, so many walkers on the Pennine Way choose to omit it, since this final stage is so long. To prevent further erosion damage, flagstones are a regular occurrence on the English side of the fence for walkers to utilise. Having been laid through the wet peat in 2013 to replace the 1989-constructed, erosion-controlling duckboards, they make for really fast progress over what was once a boggy quagmire.

You will notice the Cheviots are distinctly different to anywhere else you have traversed on the PW so far. All through Derbyshire, Yorkshire, Cumbria, and Northumberland, the fields are marked out by stonewalls or hedges with just the occasional fence dividing up larger fields. In contrast, in the Cheviots, you will not see any walls, hedges, or trees. There are only fences and most of those are post and wire. This gives the landscape a distinctly open and wild look. The Cheviots are a range of massive, rounded, hulking hills laid out in receding layers to the edge of your vision. The expansive views to distant horizons resonate with just how far and remote you have placed yourself within Great Britain. Sometimes the only signs of civilisation are the remote farmsteads nestling in the valleys below the bare hillsides. Circular stone sheepfolds (known locally as 'sheep stells') are a common landscape feature in the area.

Bypassing the Cheviot and staying on the Pennine Way, the main path turns sharply northwest with the border fence, descending below the Auchope cairn to the Auchope mountain refuge hut, the second bothy of the day. The mountain hut can be seen long before you reach it, almost teasingly so as the descent is both long and steep. In changeable weather, the descent can seem quite staggering, if not treacherous, and it is an arduous task to keep yourself moving slow and steady to prevent yourself from gaining too

What to Expect

much momentum. The awesome view ahead, however, does make up for this unexpected and burdensome descent after such a long section to complete. If you find that you are suffering with adverse weather conditions or struggling with the increased mileage on this final stage, then the mountain hut is a good place to rest overnight, leaving just a short walk into Kirk Yetholm the following morning. You can also opt to take the lower level route into the village, which again can save you both time and energy, especially if you decide to push on to the finish.

On leaving the mountain rescue hut, you will find that the ground drops before rising again to cross the Schil, climbing to 601 metres (1,972 ft.) above the College Valley. The next rise is Black Hag, where you will be moving in a northwesterly direction and will soon have to make the decision whether to take the high or low path to Kirk Yetholm. You would expect to have better views taking the high route, whereas with the lower route being shorter, you would expect it to be quicker. Whichever option you choose, descending to journey's end in the Scottish border town of Kirk Yetholm, the job is not yet finished until you have toasted your success at the Border Hotel, the official end point of the Pennine Way. Of course, there's a pub to celebrate at the end, as is the English custom. If you've attempted the entire trail, including the Bowes loop option and the side trip to the Cheviot summit, then you've just successfully walked 268 miles!

Trail Sections

While the Pennine Way in its entirety remains an epic journey and the ultimate challenge for the long-distance walker, some people may prefer to walk sections of the trail at a time. A good option is splitting the Pennine Way into more manageable sections, such as three one-week segments, particularly if you are constrained by time and/or work commitments. An example of how this could be done, including the Bowes Loop option and taking in the Cheviot summit, is as follows:

- Edale to Horton-in-Ribblesdale: 92 miles
- Horton-in-Ribblesdale to Alston: 96 miles
- Alston to Kirk Yetholm: 80 miles

It is possible to break up the Pennine Way into any number of stages depending on how many miles you intend to walk each day. Table 2 below shows an example of the route being broken into 17 stages, whereby each stage ends at a settlement with at least some overnight accommodation nearby. If one stage is walked per day, with one or two rest days, it makes for a three-week holiday that also allows for travel days at either end.

If you only have a two-week window to complete your walk and have estimated your number of trail days based on the fast paced itinerary of 14 days, then some of the shorter stages below can be doubled up to allow you to make much quicker progress along the route.

Stage	Start	End	Miles*	Km
1	Edale	Crowden	16	25.5
2	Crowden	Standedge / A62	11	17.5
3	Standedge / A62	Hebden Bridge	15	24.0
4	Hebden Bridge	Ponden	12	19.5
5	Ponden	Thornton-in-Craven	12	19.5
6	Thornton-in-Craven	Malham	11	17.5
7	Malham	Horton-in-Ribblesdale	15	24.0
8	Horton-in-Ribblesdale	Hawes	14	22.5
9	Hawes	Keld	12	19.5
10	Keld	Bowes / A66	13	21.0
11	Bowes/A66	Middleton-in-Teesdale	14	22.5
12	Middleton-in-Teesdale	Dufton	19	30.5
13	Dufton	Alston	20	32.0
14	Alston	Greenhead	17	27.5
15	Greenhead	Bellingham	21	34.0
16	Bellingham	Byrness	15	24.0
17	Byrness	Kirk Yetholm	25	40.0

* Approximate distances rounded to the nearest mile. Our basic 17 stages between settlements add up to 262 miles (with rounding). The Bowes Loop, which is approximately 4 miles, and the side trip to the Cheviot summit, which is a 2-mile round trip, are both optional and have not been included. If you opt to include these, the total distance is 268 miles.

Table 2 – Common Pennine Way Stages

Ultimately, how many stages you decide on for your own Pennine Way walk will be dependent upon your personal fitness level and hiking experience. If you have both the time and budget to allow for a more leisurely pace, then splitting up two or three of the longer stages to reduce the average daily length to around 14 miles will make for an easier and more manageable walk.

Navigation

The Pennine Way is frequently signposted, and many sections now have a flagstone path leading the way. However, there are some parts of the route that can be difficult to navigate, particularly if visibility is poor due to bad weather. There are also some sections of the path that intersect with other national trails, and the signposting is not always clear. Therefore, it is strongly recommended that you know how to use a compass and map which will enable you to stay on the right path. It is not advisable to solely rely on a GPS navigation system, which could encounter reception problems and needs to be regularly charged.

The entire Pennine Way follows a series of defined Rights of Way along which you have a legal right of access. An **acorn** is the symbol of 'Britain's National Trails' and it will be found at regular intervals along the path. This may also be used in conjunction with coloured arrows or the words 'footpath', 'bridleway', or 'byway' to indicate who can use a particular right of way. It is worth recognising the following symbols on the trail or on connecting paths and knowing who they can be used by, e.g., vehicles, horse riders, cyclists, or walkers.

- The word **'footpath'** and/or a **yellow arrow** indicates a path for use by walkers only and where, without the landowner's permission, it is illegal to cycle, ride a horse, or drive a vehicle.
- The word **'bridleway'** and/or a **blue arrow** indicates a path which can be used by walkers, horse riders, and cyclists but where, without the landowner's permission, it is illegal to drive any vehicle.
- The term **'restricted byway'** and/or a **plum arrow** indicates a path which can be used by walkers, horse riders, cyclists, and carriage

drivers but where, without the landowner's permission, it is illegal to drive any motorised vehicle.
- The word **'byway'** and/or a **red arrow** indicates a right of way that can be legally used by walkers, horse riders, cyclists, carriage drivers, and motorists.

Figure 3 – Acorn Trail Marker and Alternate Signage

Maps

In addition to a compass, it is also essential to carry a large-scale map with you when walking any long-distance trail. Not only is a map vital to support you on your journey, it can also be useful tool during the planning process. The wealth of information that a map provides can ultimately help you to decide on your own itinerary, as you are able to see exactly what options are available.

Ordnance Survey (OS) maps are extremely detailed and held in great affection by most British walkers. But they are not without problems, particularly as they are cumbersome, so can be difficult to use and fold in the field. OS Explorer maps are at a 1:25,000 scale, so every 4 cm on the map equals 1 km in the real world. They show the detail of Britain including footpaths, rights of way, open access land and the vegetation on the land. This makes them ideal for walking, running, horse riding, off-road cycling and even kayaking and climbing. To cover the areas that the Pennine Way traverses, you would require a total of eight Ordnance Survey Explorer maps, which are sheets OL1, OL2, OL16, OL21, OL30, OL31, OL42 and OL43.

The maps are printed on both sides, and the route is marked in green diamonds throughout. They are available in *Standard paper* (125g), *or Active weatherproof* editions (175g). Purchasing OS standard paper maps is the cheapest option, costing around £70 for the entire Pennine Way route. However, bear in mind that paper maps are likely to self-destruct in wind, rain, sleet, or snow. Purchasing weatherproof editions will cost you approximately twice as much, however, there are often deals on the internet if you purchase all the maps as a bundle. A plus point is that all OS Explorer maps now come with a code to allow you to download the map to a mobile device (using the OS app, available for Android and iOS). Once downloaded, you can access the maps on your device, even if you are in an area without a mobile data signal.

Harvey maps (our preferred choice) are light and compact, making them ideal for long-distance hikers concerned with space and weight in their packs. Harvey maps usually contain the entire route on one 50g map, although longer routes may be broken into sections. The Pennine Way requires three Harvey maps – the South, Central, and North sections – weighing a total of 150 grams and costing approximately £20.

The maps are made of polyethylene which is lightweight, waterproof, flexible and tear resistant, so it is quite possible to manage without a map case. Compared to the OS weatherproof maps, which can be very stiff, they can be folded easily in an endless variety of ways, so that the section of the route you need is uppermost. The Harvey trail maps present the route in a series of strip maps displayed side by side. They only show 2-3 miles either side of the trail, which is usually marked in red. If you have not used the Harvey maps before, it doesn't take long to become accustomed to the different features and symbols on their maps which are very universal.

ⓘ Due to the extra detail provided by OS maps, such as the fact that even walls and hedges are shown, it may still be valuable to look at them for the bigger picture during your planning stages.

Digital maps can be viewed on a modern smartphone using an appropriate app, which is usually provided as part of any map purchase. For our Pennine Way walk, we used ViewRanger, which worked perfectly for our digital mapping and mobile navigation needs. The ViewRanger shop provides Ordnance Survey maps for all parts of the UK as well as National Trails and selected long-distance paths.

b. Points of Interest

Whilst setting forth along the Pennine spine of England, the route's hillwalking highlights include:

Kinder Scout, a beautiful landscape and historic landmark in the Peak District National Park and focal point of the 1932 campaign that led to legislation in 1949 that established the National Parks and contributed to the development of the Pennine Way and several other long-distance footpaths. Its modest 600-metre summit plateau exerts an influence over the surrounding moors of the Dark Peak like no other.

Stoodley Pike Monument, a 121-foot obelisk atop a 402-metre (1319 ft.) high point, also known as Stoodley Pike, on the moors of the South Pennines above Hebden Bridge.

Top Withens, a ruined farmhouse said to have been the inspiration for the Earnshaw family house in Emily Brontë's *Wuthering Heights*.

What to Expect

High Force, Low Force, and Cauldron Snout, three impres-sive waterfalls along the River Tees in the North Pennines. Despite popular belief that High Force is the highest waterfall in England at 22 metres (71 ft.), several others in fact have a longer fall.

High Cup Nick, a spectacular glaciated, U-shaped chasm on the western flanks of the North Pennines Area of Outstanding Natural Beauty (AONB). Called the Grand Canyon of the Pennines, the view is one of the very best in northern England, with the valley opening up under your feet and the wide expanses of the Vale of Eden glistening in the distance all the way to the blue Lakeland hills.

Cross Fell, at 893 metres (2,930 ft.), the highest point on the Pennine Way.

Hadrian's Wall, 2,000 years old and still mightily impressive, it is one of the finest examples of Roman military architecture in Europe. Begun in 122 AD, the defensive wall runs across the neck of England for 73 miles from the banks of the River Tyne near the North Sea to the Solway Firth on the Irish Sea. Part of *Robin Hood: Prince of Thieves* was filmed at Sycamore Gap on Hadrian's Wall. It is a busy section of the Pennine Way at times as the *Hadrian's Wall Path* is an 84-mile long-distance trail in its own right.

The Cheviot, at 815 metres (2,674 ft.), the last major peak on the Pennine Way in the far north of England and highest point in the Cheviot Hills, which mark the border between England and Scotland.

Tan Hill Inn

These are landmarks that have inspired great writers, from the Brontë sisters to William Wordsworth and Charles Dickens. Aside from being wowed by the ever-changing natural scenery along the trail, you will also visit Great Britain's highest pub, the **Tan Hill Inn**, and one of the highest market towns in England, **Alston**, in the North Pennines. Local attractions are in abundance. From fabulous festivals and street parades to local farmers' markets, microbreweries, and village fêtes, there is always something happening.

If you consider yourself a 'foodie', you may well want to sample some of the delightful tea rooms and traditional fayre grown or produced locally. Similarly, if you are a history buff you might plan to walk along Hadrian's Wall, explore a famous castle, or take a ride on a steam locomotive whilst learning more about England's historic past, industries, and culture. If you have a keen interest in photography or art and want to immerse yourself in the stunning and varied landscapes, then several landmarks along the route are well deserving of more time, enabling you to capture their unique qualities on camera or canvas.

Whatever your hobby or pursuit, there will without a doubt be something to pique your interest in the surrounding area along your Pennine Way walk. Listed below are some of the lesser-known attractions both on and off the trail, as well as the gems you definitely shouldn't miss.

Hebden Bridge

Not far into the Pennine Way route, this Yorkshire market town has a reputation for being the centre of the arts due to an influx of writers, painters, and new age activists in the 1970s and 1980s. For the creatively inclined, there is plenty to explore and enjoy amongst the thriving artistic community, such as craft shops, vintage emporiums, secondhand bookshops, and organic cafes. You may even want to time your Pennine Way walk to coincide with the Hebden Bridge Arts Festival, one of Yorkshire's longest running arts festivals, which is an annual celebration of the town's creativity and unique landscape usually held late June/ early July. You could easily spend a rest day here or use the town as the start of a section hike, as Hebden Bridge is particularly accessible having regular rail services to Manchester and Leeds.

Malham Cove

If you are a fan of the Harry Potter series, then you will be excited to know that Malham Cove is where some of the movie *Harry Potter and the Deathly Hallows* was filmed (when Harry and Hermione are camping). The source of inspiration for many works of art and literature, the huge limestone amphitheatre formed through ice and water erosion during the last million years is a remarkable sight. Impressive, too, is the expansive view of the green hills of the Dales, with the 80-metre-high cliff affording a sensational view over the valley. The Pennine Way leads from Malham Village to the Cove, ascending the western grassy side up a steep rocky staircase. An extremely popular scenic spot with day walkers and tourists, you may want to spend some extra time here with your camera or sketchpad and take a closer look at the large area of deeply eroded limestone pavement rarely seen elsewhere in England.

Horton-in-Ribblesdale

With the Yorkshire three peaks of Ingleborough, Whernside, and Pen-y-Ghent on its doorstep, the tiny village of Horton-in-Ribblesdale is a mecca for walkers. The Pennine Way route takes you over Pen-y-Ghent, but a rest day can easily be spent exploring the other two peaks. You might also want to spend some time on the stunning Settle to Carlisle railway line which passes through the village. Being within the limestone area of the Yorkshire Dales, Horton-in-Ribblesdale is also popular with cavers, pot-holers, and anyone looking for beautiful countryside so take your time to enjoy the scenery.

Hawes

Situated right on the Pennine Way, scenic Hawes is Yorkshire's highest market town in the delightful Upper Wensleydale. Hawes has plenty of interesting attractions to offer, including the famous Wensleydale Cheese Factory where visitors can observe cheese making demonstrations and sample the great many varieties of Wensleydale cheese that are produced on-site. Also in town, you can see the traditional craft of rope making, pottery throwing or visit the Dales Countryside Museum, which tells the fascinating story of the Yorkshire Dales and the people who have lived, worked, and shaped the landscape there for centuries. Tuesday is market day, when the town itself takes on a lively and bustling atmosphere. There are plenty of interesting shops to explore, or you can simply enjoy a rest day and some refreshments at one of the many tea rooms and coffee shops.

Bowes

After passing the Tan Hill Inn, there are two options for the Pennine Way. One is to keep on the main route and the other is to follow the 'Bowes Loop', which takes you to the village of Bowes located above the River Greta, a substantial tributary of the Tees River. The 'Bowes Loop' can be done as a circular walk in its own right and may be an option for a side-trip. A distance of approximately 14 miles, the moorland route passes Deep Dale, Kearton Rigg, Goldsborough, Baldersdale, Cotherstone Moor, Race

Yate Rigg, Ravock, God's Bridge (a thick slab of limestone spanning the River Greta), and Lady Myres, before returning to Bowes.

Here you might also spend some time visiting the ruined Norman keep, which dominates the village. Bowes Castle, as it is known, was built upon the site of a Roman fort, Lavatris, which guarded the east end of the Stainmore Pass (its counterpart at Brough, Verteris, stood at the west end, a day's march away). Also of historical interest is the Ancient Unicorn pub itself, an old coaching inn where Charles Dickens stayed during 1838 while researching his novel 'Nicholas Nickleby'. Dotheboys Hall, the school featured in the novel, was based upon Bowes Boys Academy, which stands at the top of the front street. The headmaster of the school, William Shaw, is said to be the model for the infamous Wackford Squeers.

Alston

With a good range of facilities, Alston is an excellent option both to resupply and to take a rest day. Known as one of England's highest market towns, it has a steep cobbled main street with a distinctive market cross and many stone buildings dating from the 17th Century, which is why the town was chosen as the location for ITV productions of *Jane Eyre* and *Oliver Twist*. Follow the *Alston Town Treasure Trail* and take part in the area's first dedicated QR code Town Trail. Use your smart phone to scan the clues and then go hunting for more whilst discovering the history of the town for yourself. Alston is also the starting point for the South Tynedale Railway, England's highest narrow gauge railway, where you could take a ride on one of the lovingly restored steam and diesel engines.

If you are using Alston to top up your food supplies, you cannot get back on the Pennine Way without a visit to the local butchers to try their award winning handmade 'Cumberland Sausage'. Black pudding and Guinness is also another tasty combination that shouldn't be missed. Alston has a reputation for its delicious locally made specialities including Cumberland Mustard, and Alston Cheese, so be careful not to come away with too much to carry!

Geocaching on the Pennine Way

Did you know that all of England's National Trails now have geocaches hidden along them? Geocachers hide treasure troves in secret locations, then post clues to their whereabouts on the internet. It is the 21st century version of the traditional treasure hunt whereby adventure seekers equipped with GPS receivers can download the clues onto their device then search for the cache. Looking for them along your route will take you to some of the best views and most stunning landscapes the trail has to offer.

ⓘ If you fancy adding a bit of extra excitement to your walk, you could complete the Pennine Way geocache trail as you go. It is a free, fun way to explore a new place, or to see it from a different view.

c. Weather

The English love to talk about the weather, it's a subject we're famed for! There is a strong possibility you will experience poor weather conditions at some stage during your Pennine Way thru-hike, so it is important to be prepared for it. This will most likely be in the form of rain and cooler temperatures than you might have expected. The best time to walk the 268 miles are the summer months, from mid-May to early September, as this is when you would expect to have higher temperatures and less rainy days.

Spring and autumn are great times as well, but the weather might not be as favourable. September is the start of autumn, where temperatures start to drop and rainfall increases. It is also possible to hike the trail during the winter months, but you would have to be well-prepared for the possibility of cold, wet, and poor conditions, as winter in the north of England can be harsh and challenging.

You must also consider the real likelihood of snow on the ground and the increased risks associated with this. Whichever season you choose for your thru-hike, bear in mind that any excessive rainfall can make the ground increasingly boggy. Inhospitable trail conditions due to bad weather is not a fun experience, and can dramatically affect your progress.

Temperature

The most important measure in deciding what kind of clothing to bring is the expected temperature. Table 3 below gives the average temperatures for towns located in three of the regions you will hike through. As you can see, northern England isn't the warmest of places. With wind-chill on the summits, temperatures can still drop to freezing, even in summer. In lower regions, summer temperatures can soar into the high 20s (°C), making for a very warm day of walking.

Month	Peak District (Buxton, 245m) max/min (°C)	max/min (°F)	North Pennines (Alston, 299m) max/min (°C)	max/min (°F)	Northumberland NP (Byrness, 237m) max/min (°C)	max/min (°F)
Jan	5 / 1	41 / 34	2 / -3	36 / 26	5 / 0	41 / 32
Feb	5 / 0	41 / 32	1 / -3	34 / 26	6 / 0	43 / 32
Mar	8 / 2	46 / 36	2 / -2	36 / 28	8 / 1	46 / 34
Apr	10 / 3	50 / 37	4 / 0	39 / 32	11 / 2	52 / 36
May	14 / 6	57 / 43	8 / 2	46 / 36	14 / 4	57 / 39
Jun	17 / 9	63 / 48	11 / 5	52 / 41	17 / 8	63 / 46
Jul	19 / 11	66 / 52	12 / 7	54 / 45	19 / 9	66 / 48
Aug	19 / 10	66 / 50	12 / 7	54 / 45	18 / 9	64 / 48
Sep	16 / 11	62 / 52	8 / 5	46 / 41	16 / 7	61 / 45
Oct	12 / 6	54 / 43	7 / 3	45 / 37	12 / 5	54 / 41
Nov	8 / 3	46 / 37	4 / 0	39 / 32	8 / 2	46 / 36
Dec	6 / 1	43 / 34	2 / -2	36 / 28	5 / 0	41 / 32

Source: UK Met Office, Period 1981-2010.

Table 3 – Temperatures along the Pennines, England

For the majority of your journey, you will be on higher ground. You will experience elevations over 500m in the Peak District, Yorkshire Dales, The North Pennines, and regularly in the Northumberland National Park. In order to estimate temperatures in these areas, it is useful to use a lapse rate. As a rule of thumb, deduct 1°C per every 100m (2°F for every 1,000 ft.) of gain in elevation in the respective month you are planning your trip.

Water along the route in the rivers, lakes, and reservoirs will be very cold most of the year. In summer, water temperatures should achieve around 16-20°C in rivers and shallow or clear lakes.

Precipitation

As the weather in England can be so unpredictable, be prepared for all eventualities. For example, you may experience all four seasons in a day no matter what time of year you choose for your trip.

The Pennines, running down the centre of England, shelter the eastern regions from the moist westerly winds, casting a 'rain shadow' over the east side of England. This dry region on the downwind side of the mountainous area results in the eastern regions receiving much less precipitation than the west, which is clear from Table 4 below. You can see that the Peak District is the wettest region, but that all areas in fact receive plenty of rainy days.

Snow can fall as much as 50 days a year for the higher Pennines with an average increase of about 5 days of snow falling per year for every 100m of increased altitude. January is typically the month with the most days of snow, both falling and accumulating on the ground.

Navigation on higher ground, especially far north in the Cheviot Hills, can be difficult when there is poor visibility. Be prepared to amend your schedule if you have to allow for seriously bad weather or low cloud.

Month	Peak District (Buxton, 245m)		North Pennines (Alston, 299m)		Northumberland NP (Byrness, 237m)	
	(mm)	(days)	(mm)	(days)	(mm)	(days)
Jan	137	17	96	15	98	17
Feb	100	14	70	12	72	11
Mar	114	16	66	13	68	13
Apr	90	13	50	11	56	11
May	77	12	57	11	57	12
Jun	90	13	52	10	63	11
Jul	88	13	66	10	66	12
Aug	100	14	73	11	71	12
Sep	107	13	76	11	66	13
Oct	147	16	98	16	91	14
Nov	133	16	98	15	91	15
Dec	145	16	94	14	94	16
Annual	1,329	171	898	150	897	156

Source: UK Met Office, Period 1981-2010.

Table 4 – Precipitation along the Pennines, England

Taking all of the above information into account, our best piece of advice is to be prepared for rain at any time. The amount of rain can vary from a brief downpour to a light drizzle over hours. You would be very unlucky to find yourself in persistent heavy rainfall over several days. As clouds start to form, it is good to organise your gear so that your light rain jacket and waterproof trousers are readily available either in your front pouch or at the top of your pack. Your waterproof pack cover should also be easily accessible should the need arise to use it.

! It's important to remember that when seeking shelter during a thunderstorm, move away from freestanding trees and place your pack and other metal objects at a distance. Avoid peaks and passes and stay low to the ground among scattered boulders or trees.

What to Expect

As the impending weather is usually everyone's greatest concern, most of the accommodation along the way will have the latest forecasts and information regarding the current weather and conditions. The UK met office website (*www.metoffice.gov.uk*) is also a good place to find the latest updates for your location.

d. Camping

The Pennine Way National Trail offers a good selection of accommodation options along most of the route. However, if you are tackling the entire distance in one continuous walk, you will find the last section over the Cheviot Hills to be the longest stage without civilisation and, therefore, will be limited on places to stay overnight. Camping is certainly the most budget-friendly option if you are fine with giving up a few amenities and dealing with the elements more closely. This is what many walkers choose to do once reaching the remoter regions of northern England.

For those preferring to stay in a higher level of comfort by way of B&Bs or hotels, these options are further detailed in Section 4d *Accommodation*, as they will likely require making advance reservations.

Regulations

Unlike Scotland, where wild camping is allowed in most of the country, it remains illegal in both England and Wales. However, it is generally accepted or at least tolerated in the upland fells, with a long tradition of backpackers sleeping in the hills on suitable sites along the Pennine Way.

If you do plan to wild camp, you should pitch late, well out of sight from the trail, and leave early. You must also be prepared to follow the responsible hiker code of 'leave no trace'. This means leaving the land exactly as you found it, with no evidence of you ever having been there.

The main points to remember are:

- Take away all of your litter. including food scraps. Even when buried, it attracts scavengers, which may prey on vulnerable nesting birds or displace more specialist animals.
- Remove all traces of your tent pitch. Aim to leave your campsite in at least as good, if not better, condition than as you found it to avoid cumulative impact over time.
- Protect vegetation, especially at higher altitudes, is it is more sensitive and may never recover.
- Minimise disturbance to wildlife, particularly in the breeding season.

Do not light campfires! They not only damage deadwood habitats, which are important for the survival of certain insects and small animals, but also pose a serious risk in the uplands. Be very careful during dry periods to avoid starting an accidental fire on peaty moor and heathland when using your camp stove, as the risk is especially high. Since 1976, there have been over 350 reported incidents of wildfires destroying hundreds of acres of the Peak District moorland, the majority of which were started by arson, discarded cigarettes, barbeques, and campfires.

Human waste often has the greatest impact on the environment. Do not pollute water courses with carelessness. Take the opportunity to go to the toilet where they are provided. If nature calls and you need to go in the wild, make sure to go at least 60 metres (200 ft.) from any water source. Excavate a small, shallow hole of around 15cm (6 in.) deep, using a walking pole for example, and fill in the hole once you are finished, packing out any toilet paper used. Do not bury it, as scavengers will quickly uncover it.

Furthermore, if you need to wash, either yourself, clothing, or pots and pans it is not necessary to use soap. Even biodegradable soaps and detergents pollute streams and other water courses and should be avoided. On the Pennine Way, you will never be without a shower for more than a couple of days.

Choosing a Wild Camping Site

The remote countryside of the Pennine hills may appeal to some as perfect for wild camping. However, it should be said that conditions on the Pennine Way can often be less than hospitable with plenty of bog and mud to be found, especially in wet weather, which means finding a suitable campsite may be difficult. Unless it is raining, running water may also be hard to find depending on the time of year.

Wild Camping

If you decide to wild camp for the night, make sure you are out of sight of all roads and human habitation and are well away from the trail, then consider the climate. Remember to avoid camping in basins and dips as cold air sinks and gathers there. Likewise, moisture and dew collect the closer and level you are to water. This can lead to soaked gear or a solid layer of ice on your tent overnight. Moving just a few steps up and away from such cold-wet-air sinks can make for a much more comfortable night. It can also spare you some midge trouble.

At the same time, you want to have reasonably easy access to water for washing and cooking. Otherwise, prepare accordingly before making camp and bring extra water. Ideally, your wild camp spot will also provide wind shelter while allowing the sun to shine brightly from the east to warm and dry your tent and sleeping bag in the morning. Be sure to set up camp on durable surfaces to minimise damage to the environment.

Established Campsites

If you decide to camp the entire length of the Pennine Way, there is a great number of good established campsites en route, many of which provide full amenities so you don't have to rough it too much. From farmers' fields with just a cold-water tap and toilet, to larger campsites with electricity and full-scale amenities block, your experience can be as wild or as luxurious as you like. Hot showers, a laundry and drying room, plus the provision of a cook shelter are all very much appreciated after a day of walking in foul weather. You may even find campsites that offer Wi-Fi. If 'basic' doesn't bother you, some pubs, hostels or guesthouses along the route may offer their garden as a place to camp for a minimal sum in return for you dining in their restaurant. This is a great option if it is wet or you don't feel like cooking after all.

If you're thinking of choosing camping as your preferred option, a benefit is that you will often have the campsite to yourself or, at most, will only have to share it with a handful of people. Alternatively, if it's bad weather, you may decide to spend a little extra money and take advantage of a bunkhouse, which means you can have a more comfortable night knowing that you won't have a wet tent to pack away in the morning. The term 'bunkhouse' can be used to describe anything from a simple camping barn with nothing but a place to sleep and a log fire to keep you warm, to the home comforts of a grand hostel with double beds and a cooked breakfast provided in the morning.

Established Campsite

e. Water

Access to water should not be problematic if you fill up your water supplies each day before leaving your accommodation or campsite. Tap water in England is safe to drink unless a sign specifies otherwise. The easiest method is to carry a couple of 1-/2-litre water bottles or a water bladder (depending on your preference and style of backpack) that you can easily refill. During the day, if passing through a town or village, you could refill your water container in public restrooms (although not all meet reasonable standards of cleanliness). Alternatively, pubs/bars along the route tend to have an outside water tap where you can fill up without having to purchase anything inside. Similarly, if you are walking with a dog, pubs and cafes tend to leave a bowl of drinking water outside so your dog can also rehydrate. Shops may be reluctant to fill water bottles as they offer bottled water for sale, but you might just fancy purchasing a cold refreshment from their fridge as an alternative to water anyway.

There is no guarantee of finding running water in the hills. It can be particularly scarce on the Cheviots, so you can't rely on filling up en route. Chances of finding good water supplies in the South Pennines can also be fairly low. From our own experience, Kinder Downfall in the Peak District, for example, was merely a trickle in late June. However, regular access to water does improve significantly after crossing the Aire Gap. If you decide to split up the final section from Byrness to Kirk Yetholm into two days, take plenty of supplies of water with you, particularly if you need it for cooking as well. Water is not available at either of the mountain refuge huts and is not easily found close by. Alternatively, after the slog uphill from Byrness, you could instead camp at the top of Hen Hole where water is usually plentiful.

On the open peaty moors, there are frequent puddles of brown water, but it is not recommended to drink this unless you have a method of filtration and purification. Similarly, most streams run through farmland where water could be contaminated from the waste of livestock. In addition, water may have run off roads, housing, or agricultural fields picking up heavy metals, pesticides, and other chemical contaminants.

Therefore, filtering water before drinking it is always recommended as much of what can make you ill can't be seen by the naked eye. There are water filters that remove up to 99.9 percent of all bacteria, such as salmonella, cholera, and E. coli, and up to 99.9 percent of all protozoa, such as giardia and cryptosporidium. Water purification tablets can be used to sterilise your water bottle in the evening and will purify stream water if you run out during hot weather. The subject of water purification is further discussed is Section 6d *Food & Water*.

It is easy to become dehydrated, especially after a steep climb. Make sure you drink plenty of water, aiming to consume at least 3-4 litres during very hot days. Carrying a spare 500ml bottle in the bottom of your pack is a good idea as well as having some rehydration tablets, which can be an addition to your first aid kit. Hunger can often signal that in fact you are thirsty. A helpful rule is to make sure you drink plenty before you even set off each day, so your body is well hydrated and prepared for what is to come.

f. Safety

It's a brilliant feeling when the day finally arrives and you are able to step out into the great outdoors and explore everything around you. But it is also vital that you stay safe whilst doing so. Below is a brief overview of potential dangers that this long-distance hike may pose along with a few safety tips to help prevent unpleasant incidents.

Insects

A bothersome insect you will almost certainly come across at some point on the Pennine Way is the midge. The midge is a species of small flying insect, found in upland and lowland areas (fens, bogs, and marshes) from late spring to late summer. A single midge is almost invisible to the human eye, measuring one millimetre in length with a wingspan of less than two millimetres. They are well known for gathering in clouds and biting humans and are generally regarded as pests.

Amazingly, they can detect carbon dioxide in your breath from 200 metres away. In addition, midges are attracted to dark clothing and love boggy ground, undergrowth, and gloomy, still conditions just before dawn and sunset, which is when they are most active. (Although they can bite at any time of day.) Protect yourself from attack by using a repellent that includes the chemical DEET. If you are prone to bites and find them particularly irritating, it is a good idea to carry a midge head net in your pack. From our own experience, walking at a brisk pace also helps, as they simply can't keep up!

You must also be aware of ticks. They have become another serious pest to hikers, as they can carry several diseases, most notably Lyme disease. Also known as Lyme borreliosis, Lyme disease is difficult to diagnose and may go undetected. Early symptoms can include fever, headache, fatigue, and a skin rash. Lyme disease is treatable with antibiotics if it is diagnosed early. However, neurological problems and joint pain can develop months or years later if it's left untreated. In the worst cases, it can be fatal.

There are many different species of tick living in Britain, each preferring to feed on the blood of different animal hosts. If given the opportunity, some of them will feed on human blood, too. The one most likely to bite humans in Britain is the 'sheep tick'. (Despite its name, the sheep tick will also feed from a wide variety of mammals and birds.) Bites from other ticks are possible, including from the hedgehog tick, fox tick, and badger tick. Ticks are usually present in long grasses, woodland, and heath areas. In England, their numbers are increasing largely as a result of the warmer and wetter weather, which provides good breeding conditions. There is also a growing number of wild deer with ticks living on their skin.

The best way for walkers to avoid getting bitten is to use repellent, wear light coloured clothes, so that ticks can easily be seen, and to walk on paths, avoiding long grass or verges where possible. If you need to remove a tick, use fine tipped tweezers or a tick-removal tool to grasp the tick by the head as close to the skin as possible. Pull firmly and steadily, without twisting, as this could increase the risk of infection by prompting the tick to regurgitate saliva into the bite wound. After the tick is removed, apply antiseptic and beware of a rash. (We recommend that it is worth purchasing a tick-removal tool and keeping it in your first aid kit.)

Plants

While most plants that grow in the UK are harmless, some sting, scratch, or are poisonous, causing rashes that can be particularly bothersome. Poison ivy does not grow in the UK, but one of the most widespread plants that are the bane of many during a country walk are stinging nettles. Nettle leaves are covered in tiny, needle-like hairs. When you brush against a nettle, the hairs break off, penetrate your skin, and sting you, producing a burning/tingling sensation, itch and rash. If you get stung by a nettle, look out for a dock leaf to rub on the rash. (It is not just an old wives' tale!) Dock leaves usually grow close to nettles and are an effective natural remedy for nettle rash.

Figure 4 – Stinging Nettles and Dock Leaves

Cattle

Attacks by animals, although rare, do happen. Unfortunately, there are always hazards that can be encountered when walking though fields where there are cows. Although not having quite the same kudos as a bear (one of the main dangers when hiking in certain parts of the USA), each year in the UK there are reports of people who have been attacked or even trampled to death by cows. Most members of the public are wary of bulls, but few realise that cows, particularly those protecting newly-born calves, can also be dangerous. While such attacks are relatively rare, nationwide there have been 31 people killed by cattle in the UK in the last 10 years.

Walking with dogs and/or walking near cattle who are with young calves exacerbates your risk. A cow's natural instinct is to protect its young, and you, especially with a dog in tow, may be seen as an especially big threat. So if you are with a dog, avoid going through a field with cows entirely. Although it may be inconvenient, it's probably better to consider finding another route. Be especially vigilant if you find yourself with your dog in a field with both cows and calves. If you do feel threatened by cattle, then let go of your dog's lead and let it run free rather than trying to protect it and endanger yourself. The dog will outrun the cows and it will also outrun you!

Even without a dog, if you are walking through a field of cows, try to keep quiet and move away calmly and out of the field as soon as possible. Try not to surprise the cows. Remember that their line of vision is to the side and not straight in front. If cows get too close, do not panic and make no sudden noises. Turning quietly to face them with arms outstretched is considered to be the best approach, as is moving to the edge of the field if you can. Chances are the cows will leave you alone once they establish that you pose no threat.

Avoiding Cows

ⓘ Our best advice is that if you walk through a field of cows and there happen to be calves, think twice. If you can, go another way and avoid crossing fields. If you are involved in an incident or are hurt, you should contact the Health & Safety Executive, the local Rights-of-Way officer, and the police if the incident is serious.

Road Walking

Walking between Standedge and Hebden Bridge, an instantly recognisable landmark for both commuters and walkers alike is the Pennine Way footbridge that spans the M62, one of Britain's busiest motorways. Whilst there is the provision of footbridges and underpasses at certain prominent points along the route, there are a few sections of the trail where you will be required to cross or walk along busy roads. If there is no pavement, try to walk as far on the shoulder as possible facing the oncoming traffic, making yourself visible to approaching vehicles.

What to Expect

⚠ International travellers be reminded that in the UK, traffic is driving on the left-hand side of the road. Therefore, when crossing roads, it is advisable to look first to the right and then to the left.

General Precautions

Additional potential hazards may include dehydration, hypothermia, frostbite, sunburn, and sunstroke, as well as ankle sprain or fractures. You can minimise any potential risk by ensuring that you take sensible precautions and are thoroughly prepared. Have a map and compass and know how to read them, especially when navigating through hazardous terrain. Have the right equipment and know what to do in an emergency. Check out the Mountain Rescue's advice page[1], follow the advice, and don't overestimate your capabilities. Know your escape routes and review the path beforehand. As we have emphasised previously, always be prepared to change your plans if necessary.

If you do get into difficulties whilst walking on your own, the danger is much greater than if you have other people with you to go and get help. However, as the trail has regular walkers, it is almost certain that someone will pass by who can raise the alarm and offer assistance should something untoward occur. It is also a good idea to let someone else know your plans and itinerary, as well as carrying emergency contact details on your person.

g. Flora & Fauna

The natural landscape of the Pennines is built on foundations of grit and peat, making it a rich home for special moorland flora and fauna. Bracken, heather, sphagnum, and coarse grasses, such as cotton grass, purple moor grass, and heath rush, thrive in the acidic topsoil. These provide vital habitats for a number of species, as well as food for the large heath butterfly and black grouse. It is such a unique place that much of the watershed landscape is protected to help wildlife flourish.

---

[1] http://www.mountain.rescue.org.uk/

Unusual wildlife to watch out for along the route includes black grouse, lapwings, otters, and rare newts, as well as fell ponies in the north Pennines and feral goats in the Cheviot Hills. You might even be lucky enough to catch a glimpse of the rare Pennine finch, also known as the twite.

Peak District National Park

Heather is perhaps the plant most associated with the Dark Peak area of the Peak District National Park. Its purple-pink, honey-scented flowers are a welcome, yet short-lived, sight on the moors. Attracting a variety of pollinating insects, heather provides a late-summer nectar source for bees, such as the bilberry bumblebee, whilst also supporting species of birds, such as the skylark, twite, lapwing, curlew, short-eared owl, merlin, and golden plover. Resident in the Peak District all year round, the red grouse is also a familiar sight, as it feeds on the heather, as well as seeds, berries, and insects that nest amongst it. You will also find the park is home to adders, water voles, white-clawed crayfish, and brown hares.

When traversing Kinder Scout, you will have a good chance of spotting a bird of prey, as the plateau supports several upland breeding birds. Look out for red grouse, golden plover, twite, and waders, such as curlew and ring ouzel. The only population of mountain hares in England also thrive here. Between May and June, you will see the green hairstreak butterfly. It is widely distributed across the Dark Peak, where it favours sheltered cloughs and slopes that contain a good growth of its main larval food plant, bilberry. It can also be found along moorland roads and lanes with a narrow fringe of dense bilberry and where south-facing drystone walls provide a warm microclimate.

Yorkshire Dales National Park

The Yorkshire Dales National Park's many habitats include flower-filled meadows, moors, bogs, and small woodlands that dot the dales as remnants of formerly far more extensive forests. Important birds thrive here, as do rare plants nourished by limestone-rich soils, including wildflowers that bloom nowhere else on earth. A hundred species of nesting birds and almost 1,500 moths also call the park their home.

Even the most unobservant bird watcher cannot help noticing them from the highest fells to the depths of the vales. Skylarks hover high above the upland pastures, and lapwing, snipe, and fieldfare are all to be found. The buzzard, a medium sized bird of prey, is also a familiar sight in the national park and can often be seen using its broad rounded wings to soar in the thermals. The woodlands also harbour many small songbirds, and you will often hear, if not actually see, woodpeckers at work.

Both rabbits and grey squirrels are common animals that you will see when hiking through the Dales. Other mammals are more timid and less easy to spot, including roe deer, hare, fox, and badger. Occasionally, you may spot a native red squirrel in the woodland. The wood-mouse, mole, and vole are common but shy. There are several species of bat, which are most in evidence at dusk. Frogs, toads, lizards, and adders also live in the park.

Northumberland National Park

Northumberland National Park has some of the best bogs in Europe. Bogs might not be great to walk on, but they are vital for rare species of plants. If you hike the Pennine Way in spring, on the peat bogs you will see what looks like tufts of cotton wool swaying in the wind. Cotton grass, or bog cotton, isn't really a grass at all, but a type of sedge. It was used in the past for making candle wicks, stuffing pillows, and even dressing wounds.

Cotton Grass

Flowering bog asphodel is found on undisturbed bogs from June to August. Its bright sulphur-yellow flower spikes attract a range of pollinating insects and give the effect of a yellow carpet as far as the eye can see. Cooler and wetter conditions, such as in the high Cheviot Hills, produce a layer of peat known as blanket bog. The blanketing of the ground with a variable depth of peat gives the habitat type its name. In the Northumberland National Park, there is blanket bog up to ten metres deep! Blanket bogs are a familiar feature of the northern Pennines' dramatic upland landscape, providing a vital nesting ground for bird species such as the golden plover, dunlin, and greenshank. Approximately 40 percent of the UK's large heath butterfly population is also found on blanket bog.

Also growing here on the wet mountain slopes, you will find dwarf evergreen flowering shrubs, such as the crowberry. Crowberr has tiny, purple, starry flowers that nestle between needle-like leaves, producing small purple berries that are similar to blueberries. Another wild plant to look out for is the cloudberry, a miniature bramble with large white flowers that produces an amber-colored edible fruit similar to the raspberry or blackberry. The best time to see crowberry and cloudberry flowers is May and June. Berries are produced in the autumn and, if not picked, often persist into the winter.

> [!] In good growing conditions, it takes 10 years to create just one centimetre of peat. Trampling large areas of fragile bog exposes the bare peat, leaving it vulnerable to erosion. Walkers are always encouraged to stay on paths provided over fragile sections, such as on the Cheviot summit.

h. Other Conditions

Fire

Prior to 2012, wildfire was barely recognised as a significant hazard in the UK. With the Fire and Rescue Service now dealing with about 70,000 grassland fires a year, severe wildfire has now been added to the UK's National Risk Register of Civil Emergencies. Most wildfires in the UK are started inadvertently by humans and occur on moorlands, heaths, grassland, woodland, and agricultural land, which is why it is against the law to light any open fires without the permission of the landowner!

On some of the sections of the route, particularly as you walk through open moorland, you will see evidence of controlled burning. The heather that the moors are so famous for is kept young and vigorous by this method. If left unburned, it eventually grows long and lank. Burning is carried out by moor keepers between autumn and spring, when small sections are burned carefully on a rotational cycle, (which can be as little as seven years where there is very vigorous growth or as long as 25 years where growth is slow). These fires are very different to uncontrolled emergencies and are restricted by law to the period between 1st October and 10th April each year. Although this is nothing to be overly concerned about, it is something to be aware of when planning the dates of your hike.

Ministry of Defence (MoD) Land Holdings

A military presence, in the form of Roman legions, existed in the Otterburn area as long ago as the first and second centuries AD. In 1911, the War Office bought 7,690 hectares of land, and the artillery ranges were extended during the Second World War. Otterburn Training Area (OTA) now consists of some 22,900 hectares of land, all owned by the MoD, and is the largest single firing range in the UK. It is partitioned into three separate Danger Areas: Redesdale Range, Otterburn Range, and Bellshiels Demolition Area, and has three Outside Gun Areas. Some 30,000 soldiers use the area each year. The Cheviot Dry Training Area is to the north of these four areas.

The majority of the Training Area lies within Northumberland National Park. The rights of way in this area are accessible at all times. However, military personnel/vehicles engaging in military training activities may be encountered. The land is used for tactical training, using blank ammunition and pyrotechnics, so be prepared for sudden noises. When red flags or lamps are flown/shown and barriers are closed to denote live firing, access is restricted to roads, tracks, and paths outside the byelawed area.

[!] Although only dry training (i.e., blank ammunition and pyrotechnics) takes place within Dry Training Area, do not touch or pick up any metal objects lying on the ground.

Holidays

You should also take into consideration the designated national holidays (known as bank holidays) in the UK, where traditionally banks are closed and other shops and services may only operate on a reduced basis. There is currently a total of eight permanent bank and public holidays in England, Wales and Scotland. These include:

- Christmas Day (December 25)
- Boxing Day (December 26)
- New Year's Day (January 1)
- Good Friday and Easter Monday (with changeable dates based on the Christian calendar)
- May Day (the first Monday that falls in May)
- Whit Monday (the last Monday that falls in May, which usually coincides with a week of school holidays for Whitsuntide)
- Last Monday in August. (this holiday also falls during a school holiday – the busy six-week summer vacation period, usually from mid-July to end of August)

Choosing to hike during either the school holiday or bank holiday periods will mean an increase in traffic on the trail by way of day walkers or section hikers, as families head to the hills for some quality time outdoors. If you prefer solitude while hiking, carefully consider your travelling dates.

4. Long Lead Items

The process of planning a hike on a popular long-distance trail usually includes steps that require more lead time than others. This chapter introduces items that are generally more time-sensitive in terms of limited availability and possible cost savings and should therefore be considered early on in the planning process.

a. Permits & Regulations

Unlike in many other countries around the world, in England there is no charge for entering an area of the country designated a national park. Therefore, you do not need a permit to complete the Pennine Way National Trail. There are 15 National Parks within the United Kingdom as a whole, which are protected areas because of their beautiful countryside, variety of wildlife, and cultural heritage. On your walk along the Pennines into northern England, from Edale to Kirk Yetholm just over the Scottish border, you will certainly experience three of the most popular and most distinctive as you hike through the Peak District, the Yorkshire Dales, and the Northumberland National Park. Each area warmly welcomes visitors and provides opportunities for everyone to experience, enjoy, and learn about their special qualities.

Access & the Countryside Code

In England, despite the fact that almost all land is privately owned, there are about 936,000 hectares of open access land. This includes open country (areas of mountain, moor, heath, and down) and registered common land. People have a right of access on foot to this land, under Part 1 of the Countryside and Rights of Way (CROW) Act 2000, resulting in about 118,000 miles (190,000km) of public rights of way. This freedom to roam has brought large parts of the country's wilder landscapes within reach of walkers, climbers, runners, and wildlife enthusiasts, allowing visitors keeping to public footpaths to wander at will.

However, all visitors must adhere to the Countryside Code, which applies to all parts of the countryside in England and Wales and aims to help everyone respect, protect, and enjoy the outdoors.

The main points to remember and adhere to on your thru-hike are:

- Respect other people. Consider the local community and other people enjoying the outdoors. Always use good trail etiquette.
- Follow advice and local signs. Leave gates and property as you find them and follow paths unless wider access is available. Use gates, stiles or gaps in field boundaries if you can – climbing over walls, hedges and fences can damage them and increase the risk of farm animals escaping. When in a group, make sure the last person knows how to leave the gates.
- Co-operate with people at work in the countryside. For example, keep out of the way when farm animals are being gathered or moved and follow directions from the farmer. Don't interfere with animals even if you think they're in distress. Try to alert the farmer instead.
- Protect the natural environment. This means take special care not to damage, destroy, or remove features such as rocks, plants, and trees that provide homes and food for wildlife. Do not harm animals or disrupt their habitats, particularly during the breeding season. Also be careful not to disturb ruins and historic sites.
- Leave no trace of your visit and take your litter home. Litter and leftover food doesn't just spoil the beauty of the countryside, it can be dangerous to wildlife and farm animals. Dropping litter and dumping rubbish are both criminal offences.
- Keep dogs under effective control. Make sure your dog is not a danger or nuisance to farm animals, horses, wildlife, or other people. It is always good practice (and a legal requirement on 'open access' land) to keep your dog on a lead around farm animals and horses, for your own safety and for the welfare of the animals. A farmer may shoot a dog, which is attacking or

- chasing farm animals without being liable to compensate the dog's owner.
- Everyone knows how unpleasant dog mess is and that it can cause infections, so always clean up after your dog and get rid of the mess responsibly – 'bag it and bin it'.
- Fires can be as devastating to wildlife and habitats as they are to people and property, so be careful with naked flames and cigarettes at any time of the year. Open camp fires are illegal unless you have permission from the landowner. Sometimes, controlled fires are used to manage vegetation, particularly on heaths and moors between 1 October and 15 April, but if a fire appears to be unattended then report it by calling 999.
- You must have a rod licence to fish in England and Wales if you're aged 12 or older and should follow national and local rules (byelaws), which are aimed at protecting fish stocks and making fisheries sustainable. Be sure to check the current rules and regulations if you intend on fishing during your Pennine Way hike. The GOV.UK website[2] is a good place to find the latest updates.

b. Hiking Buddy

You may feel completely comfortable with hiking solo and enjoy the sheer amount of freedom that comes with it. You get to hike on your own schedule without having to compromise, negotiate, or consider the needs of anyone else. Yet having a hiking companion could be very beneficial to the successful completion of your thru-hike for a number of reasons as well.

If you are on a tight budget, hiking with a partner or buddy could enable you to split certain costs, e.g., for transport and accommodation. Sharing essential items of equipment can further reduce your initial costs if gear is not previously owned and additionally help minimise individual pack weight.

---

[2] http://www.gov.uk/freshwater-rod-fishing-rules/when-and-where-you-can-fish

Another clear benefit is that teamwork makes a whole lot of trail tasks much easier – from putting up a tent, fetching and filtering water, taking turns to cook, to simply having someone to take your photo in that idyllic location. It also makes your journey a shared experience that you can discuss and muse over for many years to come.

When hiking with a companion or as part of a group over a long period of time, you will inevitably develop a real sense of camaraderie. One that you may never have experienced at any other time in your life. Out there on the trail, you will hopefully be with like-minded people that share your sense of adventure and love for the great outdoors. Swapping hiking tales around the camp stove or sharing tips and inspiring others to visit places they have not yet been to over a pint or two is likely to be the order of the day.

On a long-distance hike of this magnitude, it is also very reassuring to know that you are hiking with another, particularly when hiking through the more remote regions where interactions with other walkers or communities may be minimal. Knowing there is someone else to confer with when the trail is not obvious or when you arrive at a poorly marked junction provides you with an added sense of security.

Of course, there are also disadvantages to hiking with someone else or being part of a large group of hikers on the trail. In order to have a pleasant experience, you've all got to get along, muck in, be fair, and accept a group majority, even if it's not really your thing.

If you are considering hiking with a guided group or joining a group tour, bear in mind the itinerary is usually set. You don't have the flexibility as with planning your own trip. There's no option to stay at a campsite for an extra night to take a side trip or simply deciding you will set off an hour later to stay in bed longer, especially if you have cooking duties to take care of. Group responsibilities come before your own needs. If you are someone who likes flexibility, then hiking with a guided group is probably not for you.

Similarly, if solitude is important to you, then constant company may dampen the experience and put a strain on your relationship. You will need to find some balance between hiking well together and enjoying the mutual company while still having your own space so as not to become tired of or stressed by each other. Different hiking paces can also affect the partnership. It can be frustrating to slow down to accommodate someone else's more moderate pace. Likewise, pushing harder to achieve someone else's faster pace can cause injury.

The most important thing is to know the kind of person you are on the trail and to pinpoint your strengths and weaknesses. If you are not a team player and prefer to do things your own way, you may find hiking with a companion or as part of a group both frustrating and overbearing. If you like the reassurance of having someone else with you while hiking, carefully consider all of your options before deciding who that someone else is going to be. You will be in close proximity with this person for several days, so it is imperative that you get along.

As a married couple who love to hike, we both have clearly defined roles when it comes to navigation, camp setup, and particular routines. We get along for the most part, but even with lots of experience and good organisation, we can still have our moments when we're suffering from hunger and fatigue. Taking into account all of the above, our top piece of advice is to choose your hiking buddy wisely!

c. Travel Arrangements

Getting to the start of the trail and back from the end takes some planning. Depending on where you are coming from and in which direction you plan to walk the route, there are different options to consider. Figure 5 below provides an overview of major towns and train routes across the country as well as airport connections.

ⓘ For more detailed information on UK rail routes, timetables, and current prices, a good website to look at is National Rail Enquiries (*www.nationalrail.co.uk*). This website is particularly useful as it has the latest travel news, including the location of engineering works, detailing any changes to routes and/or timetables that will affect passengers.

ⓘ Another good website to help you find up-to-date bus routes and information is Traveline (*www.traveline.info*). It is a partnership of transport companies, local authorities and passenger groups which have come together to conveniently give you routes and times for all travel in Great Britain by bus, rail, coach and ferry. You can type in the destinations you are travelling from and to, to help you plan your journey.

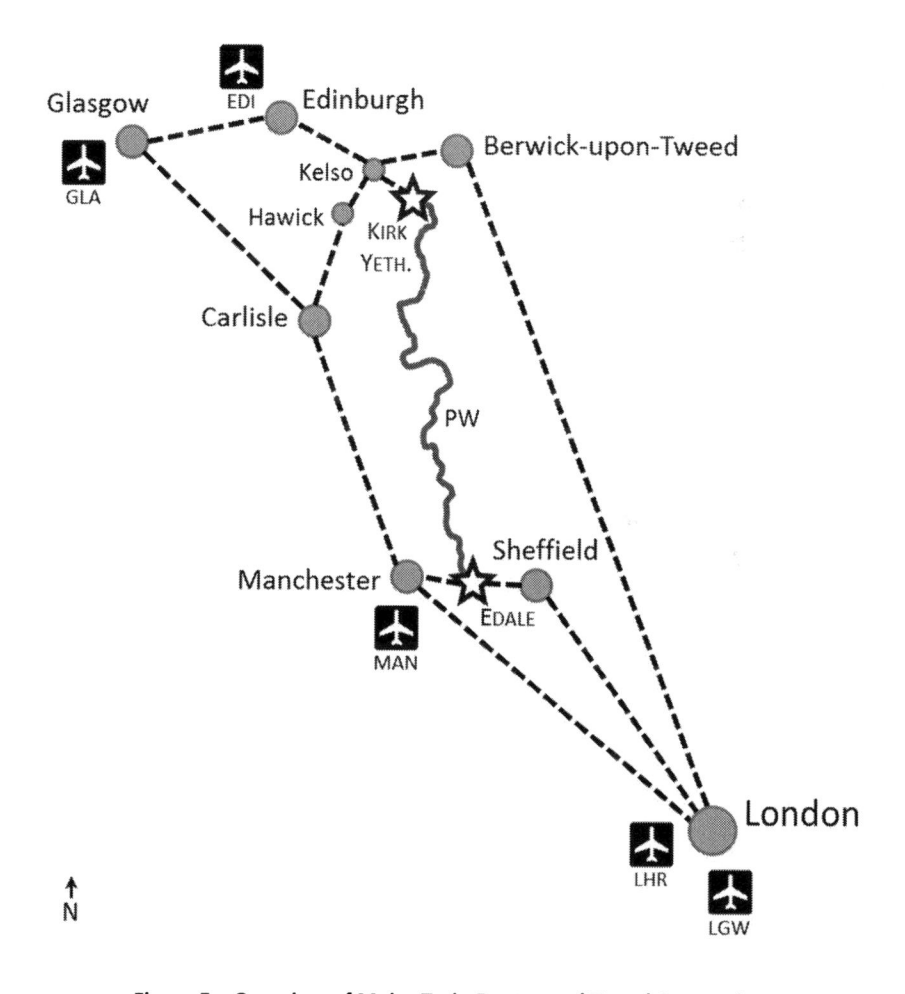

Figure 5 – Overview of Major Train Routes and Travel Connections

Long Lead Items

Starting in Edale

If you plan to hike the Pennine Way in the traditional direction, going south to north, your journey will start from the village of Edale, in the Peak District National Park, situated in Derbyshire in the Midlands of England. Due to its central location, it is very accessible by road and rail.

By Air: The nearest main airport to Derbyshire is Manchester (MAN). It is likely though that if you're from outside the UK, you'll be landing at a London airport (LHR/LGW). Once in the UK, the best way to get to the start of the trail is by rail.

By Rail: If arriving from a London airport, the best station to travel from is London St Pancras International station, which also serves continental Europe by way of the Eurostar. London to Sheffield by train takes approximately 2.5 hours. Once in Sheffield, a local train can be caught to Edale that will take about 35 minutes. If arriving in Manchester, a train can be caught from Manchester Piccadilly station to Edale that takes a journey time of approximately 45 minutes. For all, regular services operate daily.

By Bus: There are presently no bus services to Edale, but you should be able to connect to the rail services along the Manchester-Sheffield line at Hope, Hathersage, Chinley, Dore and Totley, Marple or Stockport. During the summer months, from Edale Railway station, there is a connecting bus service to Castleton at weekends and Bank Holidays.

By Car: Edale is about 45 minutes from the centre of Sheffield and Manchester, 35 minutes from Bakewell and 20 minutes from Buxton. It is most easily reached by turning north off the A6187 at Hope between Hathersage and Castleton. The main public car park in Edale is run by High Peak Borough Council which charges £5 per day on a pay and display basis.

For hiking the Pennine Way, by far the best way to get to your starting point (and returning home from the finishing point) is by public transport. This way, you need not worry about car parking (and its associated costs) or endure the tedious journey back to the car after you've completed your challenge.

If you need to connect to public transport routes to return home after completing the Pennine Way, we would recommend the following method to be the easiest.

Using Public Transport from Kirk Yetholm

From Kirk Yetholm, take the 81 bus (Peter Hogg of Jedburgh) to Kelso, then take the 67 bus (Perrymans Buses) from Kelso to Berwick-upon-Tweed. Here, you can get a direct train to London Kings Cross Station, taking approximately 3 hours 40 minutes. Rail tickets are always cheaper if an *Advance Ticket* is booked several weeks prior to departure. (This can be up to 12 weeks in advance on some main lines, so it is recommended that you sign up for ticket alerts on the relevant rail travel website.) Alternatively, from Kelso, you could take a bus to Edinburgh, if you are making your way to the airport (EDI), or take a bus to Carlisle (via Hawick), giving access to the West Coast mainline train services.

Section Hiking

If you are considering starting at an alternative point along the Pennine Way and hiking a section of the trail, then the following information regarding public transport links and availability may be of use. Whilst planning which section(s) you are going to walk and before setting off on your journey, it is always advisable to check current operating schedules and travel arrangements in case of any disruptions to services, minor delays, or temporary changes to routes.

Start	Public Transport Links
Crowden	An extra couple of miles walk down to Hadfield and there is a frequent rail service to Manchester Piccadilly that takes approximately 30 minutes.
Standedge/A62	There is a good bus service between Huddersfield and Oldham and an hourly train service between Manchester Piccadilly and Huddersfield a few miles downhill at Marsden.
Hebden Bridge	Several bus services an hour mostly running between Leeds and Manchester, plus hourly services to

	Blackpool and York. Excellent train services to Leeds, Bradford, York, Preston, Blackpool and Manchester.
Thornton-in-Craven	There's an hourly bus service between Skipton and Burnley.
Gargrave	A short journey from Leeds, trains also run to Carlisle and Morcombe. A twice daily bus service (except Sundays) stops at Gargrave running between Skipton and Malham.
Malham	There are two buses daily (except Sundays) between Malham and Skipton, also stopping at Gargrave.
Horton-in-Ribblesdale	On the Settle to Carlisle line, trains run through to Carlisle or Leeds roughly every two hours or so. Bus services only connect to nearby local villages with limited onward connections.
Hawes	Hawes has a good bus service to Leyburn with connections to the railway station at Northallerton on the main East Coast and Trans Pennine lines.
Keld	Keld has just two buses daily from Richmond. From Richmond connect to Darlington for mainline bus and rail services.
Bowes	There are two local bus services from Bowes on the 'Barnard Castle Circular' operating Monday to Friday only. From Barnard Castle connect to Richmond, then Darlington for mainline bus and rail services.
Middleton-in-Teesdale	Middleton has an hourly bus service to Darlington with a change at Barnard Castle. Be aware that buses stop at two different places in Middleton, so check which side of the road you need to be.
Dufton	With no railway station, there is very limited public transport from Dufton. For access to the West Coast mainline which has regular services to London, Crewe, Carlisle, Glasgow and Edinburgh you should take a taxi to Penrith, which is 13 miles away. Alternatively, the town of Appleby-in-Westmorland on the Settle to Carlisle line is just a few miles away.
Alston	There are bus services to both Carlisle and Haltwhistle if you need to connect with trains or buses on the Newcastle to Carlisle routes.

Greenhead	There is an hourly bus service between Carlisle, Haltwhistle, Hexham and Newcastle, with train services available from all these stations. Additionally, Apr–Oct, the Hadrian's Wall bus service provides a good service from Carlisle, Newcastle and Hexham to reach either Greenhead or the Housesteads Fort.
Bellingham	There are 8 bus services Monday to Friday (7 on Saturday) from Hexham to Bellingham and vice versa (Bus 680) operated by Go North East. Check times as the last service is early evening.
Byrness	The tiny village is connected to Newcastle by the 131 bus which runs once a day (except Sundays), operated by Peter Hogg of Jedburgh. There is also a daily National Express bus service (534) running between Glasgow and Hull that connects Byrness with major cities such as Newcastle, Manchester and Leeds.

Table 5 – Transport Links from Towns and Villages along the Pennine Way

In Table 6 below, we have listed approximate prices for travelling to and from the start and end points of the Pennine Way on public transport. Use this as a guide for making comparisons with travelling by road (hire car costs, fuel, parking) when working out your budget, to see which option is more cost-effective.

Service / Transport	Cost
Edinburgh to Edale (train)	£120
Glasgow Airport to Edale (train)	£105
Manchester to Edale (train)	£11
Sheffield to Edale (train)	£8
London Euston to Edale (train)	£80
London St Pancras to Edale (train)	£90
Edinburgh to Berwick-upon-Tweed (train)	£25
Glasgow to Carlisle (train)	£30
Manchester to Carlisle (train)	£55
London Kings Cross to Berwick-upon-Tweed (train)	£140
Kirk Yetholm to Kelso (bus)	£4

Long Lead Items

Kelso to Edinburgh (bus)	£12
Kelso to Hawick (bus)	£7
Hawick to Carlisle (bus)	£5

Table 6 – Approximate Transport Costs

d. Accommodation

The Pennine Way is well served with a variety of lodging options, so you should have no trouble finding somewhere to stay, particularly if booking in advance. Depending on your preferred accommodation type, you will find that campsites and B&Bs are the most plentiful. However, if you're prepared to walk a mile or two off the path, then your options for other accommodation types are increased.

If you have decided to do a mixture of camping and some overnight stays in low-budget accommodation, then you will find the presence of some well-placed hostels near larger villages and towns. Inevitably in some locations, particularly the remote regions further north, accommodation along the Pennine Way becomes limited. In the final stage between Byrness and Kirk Yetholm, many walkers choose to wild camp overnight to break up this long section. If you are not carrying a tent but have an adequate sleep system with you, you could consider sleeping in the Auchope bothy. Yet if this is not right for you, there is always a choice of better lodgings if you are prepared to leave the trail and rejoin it the following day by way of organised transport at designated points.

The YHA do a 'Pennine Way Booking Service' that allows you to book all of your accommodation ahead of schedule. This is great if you have a set itinerary and want to make reservations in advance so that you know your accommodation needs have been taken care of. However, this does constrain you to be in a certain place by a certain time. If you have any doubt about your schedule or prefer more flexibility, then this service may not be for you.

Sticking to your budget may be your prime consideration. However, something you should also pay attention to when looking at accommodations costs is how close/far your choice of lodging is to/from the trail. It might not seem that important during the planning stage, but adding on an extra mile or two for leaving the trail to walk into the centre of a village to reach your accommodation, for example, may not be what you need at the end of a strenuous day on the trail.

As we camped along most of the route (except in Alston where we decided to splurge on a B&B), we cannot give any personal recommendations on where to stay in terms of lodging, but we have tried to help by providing comprehensive listings of available accommodation organised by type in Appendix C. We advise that you research the options available carefully. Standards between a B&B and a hotel, for example, as well as that of different campsites, can vary greatly.

In Table 7 below, we have listed all types of accommodation available along the Pennine Way route, including camping.

Location	Camping	Bunkhouse or Barn	Hostel	B&B	Hotel or Inn
Edale	√	√	√	√	
Glossop				√	
Torside				√	
Crowden	√				
Standedge/A62	√			√	√
Mankinholes			√	√	
Hebden Bridge	√	√	√	√	√
Colden	√				
Ponden	√		√*	√	
Cowling	√			√	
Thornton-in-Craven	√		√**		
Gargarve				√	√
Malham	√	√	√	√	
Airton		√		√	
Horton-in-Ribblesdale	√	√		√	√
Hawes	√	√	√	√	√
Thwaite					√

Long Lead Items 67

Keld	✓	✓		✓	
Tan Hill	✓				✓
Bowes				✓	
Baldersdale	✓	✓		✓	
Middleton-in-Teesdale	✓	✓		✓	✓
Langdon Beck	✓		✓	✓	✓
Dufton	✓	✓	✓	✓	
Garrigill	✓	✓		✓	
Alston	✓	✓	✓	✓	✓
Greenhead	✓	✓	✓	✓	
Caw Gap	✓				
Once Brewed			✓	✓	
Stonehaugh	✓				
Bellingham	✓	✓	✓	✓	✓
Byrness	✓		✓	✓	✓
Kirk Yetholm			✓	✓	✓

*YHA Haworth (2.5 miles away)
**YHA Earby (1.5 miles away)

Table 7 – Accommodation Availability at Locations along the Pennine Way

(i) To support you in your research for choosing the accommodation that is right for you, the Pennine Way National Trails website has a useful interactive accommodation guide with listings for all budget options (*http://www.nationaltrail.co.uk/pennine-way/plan*).

5. Planning & Preparation

So you've decided to go for it and walk the Pennine Way in its entirety! 268 miles is no easy task, but with great challenge comes great reward. To help you achieve your goal, it is worthwhile investing some time and effort into carefully planning and preparing for your trip. This can be done in manageable stages, using the guidance provided in this chapter. Ultimately, you'll be able to fully submerge yourself in the great outdoors, knowing everything is properly taken care of.

a. Itinerary

The process of planning your itinerary can be broken down into two stages. The first stage includes all activities concerning long lead items, such as travel and accommodation. The resulting 'macro-plan' is the organisational frame of the hiking trip. The second stage focuses on determining the specifics of your thru-hike, such as daily distances and resupply. The resulting 'micro-plan' is your personal hiking strategy.

Macro-Planning

The flow chart below outlines the important steps in planning the logistics of your trip. The order shown was determined based on pragmatic considerations and is a mere suggestion that may be altered depending on personal preferences. Individual steps may also be omitted if not applicable.

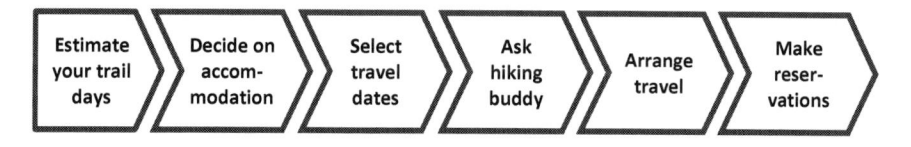

> Estimate your trail days → Decide on accommodation → Select travel dates → Ask hiking buddy → Arrange travel → Make reservations

Figure 6 – Flow Chart of Macro-Planning Steps

The first three steps address the general timing of your trip, i.e., when to go and for how long. Estimating your days on the trail gives you a good idea of the approximate duration of the trip. Be realistic about what you can achieve in terms of daily mileage. You may not have the luxury of being able to have a flexible schedule but ensure that the one you set for yourself is right for you. The next step is to decide on your preferred type of accommodation – camping, lodging, or a combination of both. This decision will likely be influenced by seasonal aspects, such as weather and public holidays, as well as your overall budget. Based on these considerations, check your schedule and determine possible travel dates.

Once you have a preliminary outline of the trip, you can use it to approach potential hiking partners, unless you plan to hike solo. You may find it easier to convince people to join you if you have a more concrete plan to present. Plus, it's usually easier to discuss and fine-tune options that have already been narrowed down compared to options that are wide open still. Once you have confirmed that the selected dates work for you and your potential hiking buddy, it is time to get started on travel arrangements, especially when you are planning to arrive from an international location.

The time of year you decide to hike the Pennine Way will ultimately determine whether or not you need to book anything in advance (e.g., transport, accommodation, side trips, points of interest). Should you choose a busy period for your walk (e.g., the height of summer/school holidays), it is wholly recommended that you book your accommodation and transport to and from the trail well beforehand.

Should you choose to walk during a quieter period, such as spring or autumn, or you have a generous timescale and want more flexibility in terms of where you stay during your journey, then reservations for accommodation may not be so time-critical. Camping, for instance, has good availability throughout the year, so it is possible to acquire a tent pitch on arrival much of the time.

ⓘ On our thru-hike, we have found camp hosts to be extremely accommodating to walkers. Even if the campsite is full, they will usually endeavour to find a spot for you if it is just for the night.

Planning & Preparation

To be able to research available accommodation options and begin booking and make other detailed arrangements, you will need a good idea of your actual hiking itinerary (i.e., daily targets). As a result, making advance reservations is a macro-planning step that partially overlaps with micro-planning activities.

Micro-Planning

The goal of this planning stage is to map out your personal hiking strategy by breaking down the overall distance of the trail into manageable daily segments. General considerations are your personal hiking speed, availability of water, the amount of food you intend to carry, when and where you plan to resupply, difficulty of the terrain, and your preferred accommodation options.

Along the Pennine Way, apart from the remote sections further north, you should never have any real difficulty with topping up your drinking water supplies or resupplying food as you will predominantly arrive at a settlement each day. To determine the difficulty of the terrain, you can use the elevation profiles provided in Appendix E, which illustrate the different gradients of the path between major towns/villages. The elevation information is particularly useful should you decide to wild camp during your trip. Pitching your tent at the base of a steep incline may provide additional protection from the elements, and having to tackle the ascent in the morning will leave the potentially easier downhill part for the afternoon when energy is starting to fade.

Essentially, planning your detailed itinerary comes down to individual hiking speed and preferred accommodation option. Below are three common itineraries that are regularly utilised on the Pennine Way. They are organised by our three budget options: camping, hostels/bunkhouses, and B&Bs/hotels. Each has a fast, moderate, and relaxed pace. To determine which hiking pace is right for you, estimate your trail days (as outlined in Section 2b *Time*) and calculate the corresponding daily mileage. In our previous example, we calculated a daily average of 14 miles (268 miles / 19 ETD), which indicates that the moderate pace itinerary might be appropriate.

ⓘ We would always recommend a relaxed pace if you have the time available, as the walk will be far more enjoyable. This also gives you additional time to explore the localities and perhaps take advantage of a zero day or two!

Example Itineraries

Budget Option 1: Camping

Location	Fast day	Fast miles (km)	Moderate day	Moderate miles (km)	Relaxed day	Relaxed miles (km)
Edale	0	0	0	0	0	0
Glossop						
Torside						
Crowden	1	16 (25.5)	1	16 (25.5)	1	16 (25.5)
Standedge / A62	2	11 (17.5)	2	11 (17.5)	2	11 (17.5)
Mankinholes						
Hebden Bridge	3	15 (24)	3	15 (24)	3	15 (24)
Colden						
Ponden			4	12 (19)	4	12 (19)
Cowling						
Thornton-in-Craven	4	24 (38.5)	5	12 (19)	5	12 (19)
Gargrave						
Airton						
Malham			6	11 (17.5)	6	11 (17.5)
Horton-in-Ribblesdale	5	26 (42)	7	15 (24)	7	15 (24)
Hawes	6	14 (22.5)	8	14 (22.5)	8	14 (22.5)
Thwaite						
Keld			9	12 (19)	9	12 (19)
Tan Hill	7	16 (25.5)			10	4 (6.5)
Bowes						
Baldersdale			10	16 (25.5)	11	12 (19)
Middleton-in-Teesdale	8	23 (37)			12	11 (17.5)
Langdon Beck			11	19 (30.5)	13	8 (13)
Dufton	9	19 (30.5)	12	11 (17.5)	14	11 (17.5)
Garrigill					15	16 (25.5)

Planning & Preparation

Location							
Alston	10	20 (32)	13	20 (32)	16	4 (6.5)	
Greenhead	11	17 (27)	14	17 (27)	17	17 (27)	
Caw Gap							
Once Brewed					18	6 (9.5)	
Stonehaugh	12	14 (22.5)	15	14 (22.5)			
Bellingham			16	7 (11)	19		
Byrness	13	22 (35)	17	22 (35)	20	22 (35)	
Kirk Yetholm	14	25 (40)	18	25 (40)	21	25 (40)	

Table 8 – Fast, Moderate & Relaxed Pace Itineraries for Budget Option 1: Camping

If Day 1 seems too ambitious, it is possible to wild camp discreetly on the Kinder Plateau. Similarly, it is possible to wild camp at other points along the route, which from our own experiences are described in Chapter 7b *Go*.

Budget Option 2: Hostels, Camping Barns & Bunkhouses

Location	Fast		Moderate		Relaxed	
	day	miles (km)	day	miles (km)	day	miles (km)
Edale	0	0	0	0	0	0
Glossop						
Torside						
Crowden*	1	16 (25.5)	1	16 (25.5)	1	16 (25.5)
Standedge / A62						
Mankinholes	2	22 (35)	2	22 (35)	2	22 (35)
Hebden Bridge					3	4 (6.5)
Colden						
Ponden**	3	16 (25.5)	3	16 (25.5)	4	12 (19)
Cowling						
Thornton-in-Craven***	4	12 (19)	4	12 (19)	5	12 (19)
Gargrave						
Airton						
Malham			5	11 (17.5)	6	11 (17.5)
Horton-in-Ribblesdale	5	26 (42)	6	15 (24)	7	15 (24)
Hawes	6	14 (22.5)	7	14 (22.5)	8	14 (22.5)
Thwaite						
Keld			8	12 (19)	9	12 (19)
Tan Hill	7	16 (25.5)			10	4 (6.5)

Planning & Preparation

Location							
Bowes							
Baldersdale			9	16 (25.5)	11	12 (19)
Middleton-in-Teesdale	8	23 (37)	10	11 (17.5)	12	11 (17.5)
Langdon Beck			11	8 (13)	13	8 (13)
Dufton	9	19 (30.5)	12	11 (17.5)	14	11 (17.5)
Garrigill					15	16 (25.5)
Alston	10	20 (32)	13	20 (32)	16	4 (6.5)
Greenhead			14	17 (27)	17	17 (27)
Caw Gap						
Once Brewed	11	23 (37)	15	6 (9.5)	18	6 (9.5)
Stonehaugh						
Bellingham	12	15 (24)	16	15 (24)	19	15 (24)
Byrness	13	22 (35)	17	22 (35)	20	22 (35)
Kirk Yetholm	14	25 (40)	18	25 (40)	21	25 (40)

* Alternate accommodation required as the hostel at Crowden only accepts large groups.
** YHA Haworth (2.5 miles away)
*** YHA Earby (1.5 miles away)

Table 9 – Fast, Moderate & Relaxed Pace Itineraries for Budget Option 2: Hostels, Camping Barns & Bunkhouses

Budget Option 3: B&Bs, Guesthouses & Hotels

Location	Fast		Moderate		Relaxed	
	day	miles (km)	day	miles (km)	day	miles (km)
Edale	0	0	0	0	0	0
Glossop						
Torside	1	15 (24)	1	15 (24)	1	15 (24)
Crowden						
Standedge / A62			2	12 (19)	2	12 (19)
Mankinholes						
Hebden Bridge	2	27 (43)	3	15 (24)	3	15 (24)
Colden						
Ponden			4	12 (19)	4	12 (19)
Cowling	3	17 (27)				
Thornton-in-Craven						
Gargrave			5	17 (27)	5	17 (27)
Airton						
Malham	4	18 (29)	6	6 (9.5)	6	6 (9.5)

74   *Planning & Preparation*

Horton-in-Ribblesdale	5	15 (24)	7	15 (24)	7	15 (24)
Hawes	6	14 (22.5)	8	14 (22.5)	8	14 (22.5)
Thwaite						
Keld			9	12 (19)	9	12 (19)
Tan Hill	7	16 (25.5)			10	4 (6.5)
Bowes						
Baldersdale			10	16 (25.5)	11	12 (19)
Middleton-in-Teesdale	8	23 (37)			12	11 (17.5)
Langdon Beck			11	19 (30.5)	13	8 (13)
Dufton	9	19 (30.5)	12	11 (17.5)	14	11 (17.5)
Garrigill					15	16 (25.5)
Alston	10	20 (32)	13	20 (32)	16	4 (6.5)
Greenhead	11	17 (27)	14	17 (27)	17	17 (27)
Caw Gap						
Once Brewed			15	6 (9.5)	18	6 (9.5)
Stonehaugh						
Bellingham	12	21 (34)	16	15 (24)	19	15 (24)
Byrness	13	22 (35)	17	22 (35)	20	22 (35)
Kirk Yetholm	14	25 (40)	18	25 (40)	21	25 (40)

Table 10 – Fast, Moderate & Relaxed Pace Itineraries for Budget Option 3: B&Bs, Guesthouses & Hotels

b. Food

Food should not be underestimated in its ability to revive energy and keep spirits up. Looking forward to a good meal is motivational, and having a satisfied stomach lets you fall asleep more contentedly at night. If you are camping and choosing to cook your own meals as opposed to the more expensive option of dining out, then putting your efforts into planning and preparing balanced meals with a lot of variety is well worth the effort. There's nothing worse than knowing you will have to eat something that's not the least bit enjoyable. You still have the option of seeking refuge in a pub and having a home-cooked meal prepared for you once in a while, particularly if it should rain or you just don't feel like cooking on a particular evening.

On the Pennine Way, with the exception of the final 25-mile section between Byrness and Kirk Yetholm, it is possible to purchase food daily along the route. Deciding what food to carry based on weight, nutritional value, and calorie distribution, as well as ease of preparation can involve a lot of work. One of the great things about hiking in England is that this step in the planning process is not necessarily required. Whether you are passing through a small village or a large town, there will almost always be the option of either a small local shop, cafe, or pub where you can get food and drink.

If you are taking a more flexible approach, you may wish to carry a few days' rations at a time to allow for spontaneous decisions. This could be taking side trips to specific areas of interest or wild camping away from settlement areas. Similarly, you may not reach your target destination due to minor injury or fatigue and may have to set up camp early. Ultimately, being prepared for all eventualities and having some provisions in your pack to allow you to cook at least a couple of high calorie, filling meals is always a good idea.

If you decide on carrying several days' worth of meals in your pack, below are some guidelines for choosing your food (refer to Appendix B for a comprehensive list of meal suggestions):

- Weight: your food should be as dry and light as possible (incl. packaging)
- Nutritional value: combine foods to ensure an adequate supply of vitamins and minerals
- Calorie distribution: balance approximately 15% protein, 60% carbohydrates, and 25% fat per meal
- Non-perishable: your food must not spoil for a week or longer in rather warm and humid conditions
- Easy preparation: save gas, time, dirty pots, and nerves after a long day of hiking

Two factors are particularly important to consider when determining how much food to bring – calorie value and space. Your meals should provide approximately 1.5-2 times the calories you usually consume per day. Calculate higher calories when in low temperatures and vice versa. Additional hunger can be satisfied with snacks. If you are carrying all of your own gear, including a tent and cooking equipment, then space is at a premium. Dealing with restrictions on space usually overrules weight issues. The less space you have the less water and air content should be in your food packaging. This makes for a dense nutritional value.

> ⓘ As a rule of thumb, you should aim for about ½-1kg (1-2 lbs.) of food per person per day.

In order to avoid space issues, it helps to repackage your food into single servings, let out any air, and cut off excess packaging. Zip lock bags work well. They can be labelled and reused for packing out waste. If you choose to bring a sealable food canister, try to make layers of meals per day rather than locking in all breakfast items at the bottom. This makes accessing your food more convenient. Furthermore, stack the most perishable food items at the top of your canister for early consumption.

In addition to your main meals, well-chosen snacks and supplements provide valuable nourishment. As temperatures rise, it is vital to replenish electrolytes, such as sodium, chloride, potassium, magnesium, manganese, and calcium, on a consistent basis. High water intake without electrolyte replacement over many hours can lead to hyponatraemia, a life-threatening condition where your body does not have enough salts to function. Adding salty snacks (crisps, salted nuts, savoury crackers, or pretzels) and/or supplements to your trail diet helps avoid electrolyte imbalance.

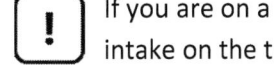

> ❗ If you are on a low sodium diet, ask your doctor if a higher sodium intake on the trail would be appropriate for you or not.

As you plan your meals, mind the respective cooking times and utensils needed for preparation. Anything that requires boiling for over ten minutes can be bothersome. Similarly, in-camp preparations, such as cutting, peeling, and mashing, or meals that require a lot of attention and flipping with spatulas can be a hassle after a long day of hiking. Many hikers plan their meals so that the only cooking gear required is a small gas stove, one pot, and one spoon. Nevertheless, whatever meals you decide to go with, bring along adequate equipment and know your own patience.

> [!] After preparing food at camp, do dishes at least 60 metres (200 ft.) from your campsite and any water source. Use biodegradable soap and scatter dishwater afterwards. Also, be sure to pack any leftovers and store your food securely and at a safe distance away from camp to avoid attracting any unwanted visitors.

Despite the suggestions given above, you may have already changed your mind about carrying your own food and cooking. It could be that you are quite content with dining out during your walk. After all, sampling some traditional fayre and visiting a pub or two is all part of the experience. (Just keep in mind when you are working out your budget that purchasing all meals en route will not be cheap!)

You may decide to alternate your food strategy depending on the campsite you are staying at, the arrival time, and the difficulty of the day ahead. For example, scenic spots and slow days might invite you to enjoy a relaxing morning coffee or spend a long evening with celebratory dining. In summary, your food strategy is a matter of your personal preference, the tightness of your schedule, access to food, your resupply strategy, access to gas, and ultimately what your overall budget will allow.

c. Resupply

Unlike other long-distance hikes where you may be in the wilderness in the truest sense and several days away from civilisation, on the Pennine Way you will predominantly arrive at a settlement each day, thereby enabling you to purchase daily food rations as you go. Where shopping options may be limited in the remoter sections of your walk such as the Cheviot Hills, you can plan accordingly and carry snacks/meal options with you to allow some flexibility.

Although small village grocery stores generally have a limited selection of easy-to-cook foods, several larger villages and towns have at least one large supermarket, offering you a better choice as they stock a wider variety of goods. In addition, when hiking through villages and towns, you may pass a local butcher, which is a good place to get fresh meat or snacks for on the go, such as pies and pastries. There is also the possibility of getting fresh eggs each day as you pass by local farms. Eggs can be considered a luxury item when hiking, but if you can carry them successfully, they make a good hearty breakfast in several forms.

On some remoter sections of the Pennine Way, you may find an unexpected but thoughtfully placed 'honesty box'. This is where some kind-hearted soul has taken it upon themselves to manage and stock a container with goodies for the benefit of any hiker walking past. The contents can vary but may consist of chocolate bars, cans of fizzy drinks, cakes, and boxes of eggs. There may even be the occasional beer! The goods are not free however. They are competitively priced and rely on the walker being honest and paying for anything he/she has taken by putting the relevant money in a tin. What is great about the honesty boxes is that they usually appear at times when your energy is drained and a treat is very much desirable. From our own experience, they certainly serve as a good rest and resupply stop to get you motivated and reenergised for the next section of your walk.

Early on in your walk, a gem just off the Pennine Way route is 'May's Aladdin's Cave'. Aptly named, it is a tiny shop stocked to the brim with everything you could possibly wish for as a hiker, which is perfect if you need to make a resupply stop when leaving Jack's Bridge to save you walking further into the town of Hebden, which is off-route. The village farm shop also provides basic camping for Pennine Way walkers should you want to end your day here and make it an overnight stop.

Located between Hadrian's Wall and Bellingham, a place also not to be missed is Horneystead Farm. It is a DIY refreshments barn right on the Pennine Way route, which is basically a walkers' service station complete with comfy chairs, tables, and heaters for drying wet clothes. Hot and cold drinks and snacks are provided with an honesty box making it the perfect place for a rest stop after a tiring morning.

Table 11 below will assist you with your food and resupply planning. It indicates the availability of food stores and eateries along the Pennine Way. Also included are the locations of post offices, cash machines (ATM), and outdoor gear shops, should you require them during your long-distance walk.

Location	Post Office	Food Store	Eatery/ Food Place	Outdoor Equipmt.	ATM/Cash Machine
Edale		✓	✓		✓
Crowden*		✓			
Standedge / A62			✓		
A672 Crossing			✓		
Hebden Bridge	✓	✓	✓	✓	✓
Colden		✓			
Cowling	✓	✓			
Thornton-in-Craven	✓				
Gargrave	✓	✓	✓		✓
Malham	✓	✓	✓		
Horton-in-Ribblesdale		✓	✓		
Hawes	✓	✓	✓	✓	✓
Thwaite			✓		
Keld*		✓			
Tan Hill Inn			✓		
Bowes	✓				
Middleton-in-Teesdale	✓	✓	✓		✓
Dufton			✓		
Bellingham	✓	✓	✓	✓	✓
Byrness			✓		
Kirk Yetholm	✓	✓	✓		

* Campsite shop

Table 11 – Locations of Important Village/ Town Facilities on the Pennine Way

d. Training

The Pennine Way may be your greatest challenge to date so it is important that you prepare yourself both physically and mentally. Being in excellent shape before you start a long-distance hike makes a big difference as to how much you enjoy the experience and whether or not you successfully complete it. Proper training therefore will significantly increase your chances of success, improve the quality of your days on the trail, and decrease the chances of overuse injuries.

Mental Preparation

The right attitude in every phase of the process is just as important as proper physical and logistical preparation. From the moment you make the decision, through the weeks of planning your trip, to the final day on the trail, maintaining an open mind and a resilient attitude in coping with obstacles is essential. At any given point, you may be confronted with fatigue, anxiety, or doubt. In those moments, remind yourself that even the smallest steps in the right direction will help you achieve the goal eventually.

Physical Preparation

Endurance and strength are indispensable assets when it comes to going the full distance of a thru-hike. If your body is not used to walking long distances on a daily basis while carrying the extra weight of up to 18kg (40 lbs.), it will need proper conditioning. Individual workout needs may vary based on age, health, current fitness level, and other factors. However, the general intention is to get your body moving and comfortable with being active early on, and then gradually increase the intensity.

A good training routine will incorporate cardiovascular exercises and weight lifting elements. Go hiking frequently and participate in other forms of aerobic fitness like cycling, swimming, running, or group fitness classes. This will not only increase your endurance, but also build confidence and momentum for your adventure. Additionally, exercise with light to medium weights to strengthen shoulder and back muscles.

As your fitness level develops, it is crucial to add weight to some of your cardio exercises to simulate the backpack you will be carrying on the trail. Carrying a backpack over rough terrain uses your core, leg and foot muscles for balance in a way that everyday walking does not. Begin wearing an empty pack, then a partially weighted pack, and eventually the equivalent weight of what you plan to carry during the trip. For an even better training effect, you could gradually progress your practice hikes to steeper terrain. These 'training walks' are invaluable, particularly if you have purchased new gear. You can adequately put it to the test and implement any changes to your kit should this be necessary.

Give yourself plenty of time for training – a few months at least. Overtraining can lead to injury so take it slowly. You are always better off starting a bit less fit than you would have liked, but injury free. Undertaken gradually and over similar terrain, your training should culminate in 15-mile walks with a fully loaded backpack if you are intending on tackling the entire distance of the Pennine Way in one go.

Hiking Style

It is helpful to adopt a good hiking style to use your energy efficiently and to keep strains to your joints and tendons to a minimum. Pay particular attention to the following three habits on the trail:

Hike at a Sustainable Pace

Regard the Pennine Way as an ultra-marathon, not a sprint. From an athletic point of view, this means that you need to keep your metabolism and energy conversion in an aerobic state. In brief, aerobic metabolism means that your muscles are receiving enough oxygen from your lungs, sufficient fuel through your bloodstream, and have enough time to dispose of by-products from burning the fuel (i.e., exercising), especially lactic acid.

The aerobic state or respiration is usually the sweet spot for your body to process its energy, from a nutritional intake as well as fat storage perspective. Keep in mind that even very fit people have an average body fat level of 5-15 percent. That means that a 75kg (165 lbs.) person would have around 8kg (17 lbs.) of fat which contain approximately 56,000 calories, enough caloric energy for over 20 days. This body fat is a valuable reserve you should tap into on the trail in order to keep your packed food weight low and potentially reduce your body weight as a pleasant side effect. Maintaining a sustainable pace allows you to do just that.

Your personal sustainable pace will vary depending on your level of fitness, the altitude, weather, and time of day. However, any variation should usually not be more than approx. +/-20 percent of your average, unless there is an exceptionally difficult/steep section. Finding your personal sustainable pace is simple. It is the pace at which you breathe deeply, but not rushed, you may sweat, but never excessively, and you don't feel the need to take a break before an hour or longer. Not taking a break but rather maintaining a steady pace is essential to keep your metabolism up and you on your feet longer.

Remember, your personal sustainable pace is personal. It can be faster in the morning, when it is still cool, and slower at a sun-beaten incline. It's okay to keep a slow "one Mississippi – step – two Mississippi – step" rhythm. In the end, a slow but sustainable pace will be the fastest, because you will feel less fatigue and need less rest/recovery time.

Take Small Steps

In line with maintaining a sustainable pace, small steps avoid stress peaks for your muscles, reduce force of impact on your joints and reduce the likelihood of a misstep injury. The Pennine Way route has varying surface conditions. At times, you have well placed steps on well-trodden trails, other times you are walking over boggy moorland or stony ground, which may cause stress on your feet. Wearing well-cushioned trail shoes or hiking boots will help with traversing the varied terrain.

The best surfaces are flat, firm, and not too hard. Tarmac/concrete are the hardest walking surfaces, so road walking, for instance, tends to have the most impact on your feet and can also be a source of high stress on joints. Taking small conscious steps keeps the strain on your muscles at a low level, avoiding muscle ache. Especially, when hiking uphill with a full pack, small steps will reduce exhaustion and extend your range. Opposite to this, descending with a full pack causes many hikers to suffer from knee and ankle pain. The larger the step, the greater the vertical drop and, hence, impact to your joints. Also, small steps are less likely to go wrong. A small step has less momentum that could potentially cause you to twist your ankle or slip on loose gravel.

Always Place Your Feet in the Direction of the Slope

The last recommendation is especially important when hiking downhill. Look at the direction and angle of the slope. Always place your foot so that it is in-line with the direction of the slope. If the path is going straight down the mountain, your toes should also point straight down. If there are switchbacks, you should adhere to the respective slope of the trail.

Why? Think of it this way, if you do slip, you want your toes to shoot up/forward. You may land on your bottom or backpack, but both are usually padded. If you had your foot at an angle to the slope and slipped, your body weight would follow the slope and push forward, twisting your ankle and potentially causing a painful injury at an inconvenient location. So remember, always point your toes to the slope!

Trekking Poles

Various forums and literature state that the proper use of trekking poles may increase your daily distance by up to 25 percent. Regardless of whether or not this is accurate for you, there are some definite advantages to hiking with poles that are a little easier to grasp:

More stability and balance – When carrying a heavy pack, especially one in which the weight is not evenly distributed, you can easily lose your balance. Having two extra points of contact with the trail, you are less likely to slip in the first place, and slips are less likely to turn into falls. On your Pennine Way walk you may have to cross streams on stepping stones and traverse several boggy moors. Your poles are especially handy there to test the solidity of the ground and to help keep you upright.

Less stress on joints and muscles – In addition to preventing falls, trekking poles reduce the impact of hiking on legs, knees, ankles, and feet. When going downhill, they can be used to slow down your forward movement, reducing the compressive force on your joints, in particular your knees. On steep ascents, poles help hikers maintain forward momentum by recruiting upper body muscles to the task, reducing the strain that would ordinarily be absorbed by the lower body alone. This is particularly relevant when coming down the fells along the Pennines.

> ⚠ When navigating steep terrain, it is important to find the right balance. Make sure not to overly strain your shoulders while trying to provide relief to your legs.

The propulsion aspect of the trekking poles is also important. Even though your legs will undoubtedly be doing most of the work, your upper body can support them. Walking with poles can help you establish and maintain a consistent rhythm, which can reduce overall fatigue and increase your speed. This is especially true on flatter, non-technical terrain. If you do decide to use trekking poles, make sure to familiarise yourself with the right technique. (Various tutorial videos can be found online that provide excellent guidance.) In addition, allow yourself phases of rest from using your poles.

> ⓘ Before taking trekking poles on the Pennine Way, it is very helpful to try them out on a nearby trail to see how they feel. Practice the motion which is a little different from your usual one. If you cannot get comfortable or find that poles cause additional exhaustion, leave it at that. Especially, if you already have problems with your shoulders or wrists, poles may cause unnecessary stress.

6. Gear

This chapter is intended as a general guide to support each of the itineraries suggested in this book. Your choice of gear may very well impact upon the overall success of your thru-hike so it should be considered carefully, but this does not mean it should break your budget. Before buying expensive outdoor gear, take time to consider your needs and available alternatives. Ultimately, what you need is equipment that will keep you warm, dry, safe, and comfortable under any circumstances you can realistically expect to encounter on your journey.

a. Clothing

When hiking during summer, you should find that northern England is generally warm. Expect daily temperatures to be in the low 20s (°C) on average. Once the sun goes down, evening temperatures will be cooler with the possibility of dropping into single digits.

Daytime – 8:00 AM to 8:00 PM

During the day, hiking in shorts or lightweight hiking trousers and a T-shirt (of lightweight, moisture wicking, stretchy material as opposed to cotton) is perfectly adequate. Remember the mantra – layer, layer, layer. As a general rule, a thin layer of wool or man-made fibre next to the skin to wick moisture away is perfect as a base layer. On top of this, a mid-weight or heavier layer, such as fleece, should be worn for insulation on a cooler morning around camp. Wind protection should be a lightweight wind-shell. A good habit is to keep an insulating layer and a wind jacket easily accessible at the top of your pack, should the weather turn cooler. Similarly, always ensure your waterproof clothing is readily available, too. Always carry a good breathable waterproof jacket with hood and trousers.

ⓘ If possible, opt for shirts and jackets without seams on the shoulders to avoid rubbing and pressure points from your pack straps.

Another essential piece of kit is sun protection for your head/face in the form of a cap or a wide-brimmed hat. You may prefer to shade your neck also by choosing a hat with a neck flap. If you choose to hike in shorts, you may wish to consider midge protection in the form of a midge repellent spray, which you can buy in outdoor gear shops and pharmacies along the path. Also be aware of nettle stings and scratches to legs from bushes/undergrowth. The same applies if you prefer to wear short sleeve tops in hot weather. Wearing a long sleeve top to cover your skin will provide you with good sun protection at higher elevations.

Night time – 8:00 PM to 8:00 AM

In the evening, you may wish to change into something more comfortable, e.g., long trousers and a long sleeve top. Alternatively, you could put on your sleepwear (thermal leggings and long sleeve top), thereby reducing the need for several sets of clothing. Once you have set up camp, if you are sitting around in the evening after sunset, you will most definitely need a warmer layer, such as a fleece jacket or a synthetic insulated jacket, to keep out the cold. Also for the evening, it may be a good idea to ensure you have a warm hat, such as a beanie, as well as gloves. For the temperature ranges you will encounter on your trip, a fleece or synthetic insulated jacket will be more than adequate for most people. A down jacket may be too warm and is not suitable for the damper climate of northern England in summer. We carried a lightweight vest/gilet as an extra mid-layer.

Additional Clothing

When considering underwear options, synthetic underwear is preferable as it is light, quick-drying, and has good breathability. You should avoid cotton as it doesn't wick moisture very well and is also known for chafing badly against the skin. Merino wool underwear is an excellent alternative, but is generally more expensive than synthetic materials.

When considering outer layers for your trip, a good quality mid-weight waterproof jacket (hard shell) will be suitable. This can also double up as a wind jacket. Good rain jackets will cost you money, but this is an area where we feel your money will be well spent. You might find a cheaper jacket that will do the job, but if it decides to rain persistently over several hours, you may regret choosing cost over performance. It's better to be confident about the reliability of your gear and not to have to worry about putting it to the test!

We would recommend on all hiking outings that you include a sun hat (cap, wide brimmed hat), as well as cold weather head gear. You may also like to include a multifunctional scarf and ear warmers/ear muffs as part of your all-weather kit. These are really useful on cool mornings or evenings when you are sitting around camp, so well worth carrying the extra few grams.

Inside your sleeping bag, it is never advisable to sleep with your skin directly against the bag. Your choice of sleepwear is very personal, but your key priorities should be comfort and warmth. Our preferred choice of sleepwear is merino wool leggings and a long sleeve top. We also add a silk liner to our kit. A silk liner protects your sleeping bag as well as giving you an extra layer of insulation, generally adding a couple of degrees to your bag.

It is a good idea to have an additional pair of shoes to wear around camp. Lightweight camp shoes such as flip-flops or sports sandals are really useful as changing out of your trail shoes/hiking boots, even for a short period of time, allows your feet to breathe and have a rest. They are also good for doubling up as footwear in public showers.

My preference as a woman is to hike in synthetic leggings (e.g., running compression leggings), which are really comfy to walk in. They are flexible and do not have a zipper or button that can rub or become uncomfortable/bothersome whilst wearing a hip belt.

Washing Clothes

When considering your clothing options, keep in mind that the lighter your load, the more comfortable your walk. If you can double up on the function of anything, do so. Laundry facilities are available at various points along the route, particularly if you are staying in hostels, hotels, or B&Bs, so you may have the opportunity to wash and reuse items.

Example Clothing List

This was our clothing packing list (each):

3 pairs of hiking socks	1 long sleeve t-shirt
1 pair of bed socks	2 short sleeve t-shirts
3 underwear	1 gilet (waistcoat)
1 long sleeve top (sleepwear)	1 fleece jacket/wind jacket
1 leggings (sleepwear)	1 lightweight thermal jacket
1 hiking trousers/leggings	1 rain shell
1 shorts	1 beanie/woolly hat
1 cap/sun hat	1 pair of gloves

b. Hiking

Basic hiking gear usually consists of appropriate footwear, additional ankle and leg protection, a fitting and well-balanced backpack, and optional trekking poles. This section provides an overview of available options and features, discusses pros and cons, and offers advice on how to carefully choose and properly fit individual items.

Shoes & Boots

If you are going to be successful with walking 268 miles, then you need to carefully consider your choice of footwear as it will be the most stressed piece of gear on your trip. Any good shoe has a thick, cushioning sole with non-slip tread. Beyond that, each of us has our own individual needs for footwear. A lot of which shoe or boot is right for you depends on how strong and flexible your ankles are, how much weight you plan on carrying, the size and shape of your feet, and the terrain you plan to cross, as well as just your preferences and what you feel most comfortable in. There are three typical styles: hiking boot, hiking shoe, and trail runner. They each have their individual assets and drawbacks as outlined below.

| Hiking Boot | Hiking Shoe | Trail Runner |

Figure 7 – Hiking Shoes & Boots[3]

Hiking Boots provide more stability overall. A well-fitting boot is snug, supports the ankle and reduces the risk of twisting on a slight misstep. With more contact area, the foot can be less likely to move back and forth in a good boot. The high rising sides also offer ankle protection from hitting rocks and prevent grass seed and grit from entering the boot. Other advantages are warmth and water resistance. Drawbacks of boots are the greater weight, stiffness (and hence resistance during walking strides), chances of blisters from ill-fitting boots, and lower breathability.

Hiking Shoes combine the grip stability of a good boot with more flexibility. The low cut allows more mobility and light mesh uppers enable moisture wicking. Watch out for firm heel support and a plastic cap to protect your toes. Different brands have various lacing systems, some enabling great fit in minimal time. Hiking shoes are lighter than boots and generally feel less restrictive while still providing sufficient stability. Drawbacks are the reduced ankle support, reduced water resistance, and incompatibility with crampons, although the latter is irrelevant for the Pennine Way, unless hiking during the winter months. As the Pennine Way harbours the real possibility of walking through boggy ground at some stage, hiking shoes lined with a waterproof membrane to help keep your feet dry, although making the shoe slightly heavier, is a better option for this walk.

---

[3] Sketches of Asolo boot and Salomon shoes

Gear

Trail Runners go one step further regarding agility and lightness, weighing about as much as a conventional running shoe. In order to save weight, trail runners usually provide less cushioning than hiking shoes, while still offering good tread and lots of grip. Upper materials are mostly breathable, light meshes, offering more support than running shoes but far less than a boot. Quick lacing systems are also available. Generally, trail runners are aimed at people going for a run in the mountains or woods, not necessarily long hiking trips with heavy backpacks. Drawbacks are low overall support and cushioning, plus the soles wear out much quicker walking on hard surfaces such as stony trails or tarmac.

Put your feet first! Today, the trend is away from the expensive, heavy, ankle-high leather hiking boots. Whichever shoe or boot you decide to go with, make sure you are confident about your choice. It should provide adequate support to you and your pack weight, wick moisture from your feet, not be too heavy and tiring, have a well-cushioned sole, and most importantly a padded inside that does not cause blisters, as blisters can ruin even the best-laid walking plans.

Shoes can make or break a trip, so make sure they are a perfect fit. Remember that feet swell during walking, so ensure your shoes are roomy. When shopping for new hiking shoes, wear the same type, thickness, and number of socks you'll be using when on the trail. If possible, try on new shoes at the end of the day, when your feet are puffed up to hiking size.

ⓘ Buy shoes at least half a size bigger than you normally would. This will allow you to wear padded socks for additional comfort and prevent your toes from hitting against the tips when descending.

It is important that you never buy new hiking shoes just before you start a trip! We strongly recommend using your prospective shoes on at least a few training hikes to break them in and see how they perform. Walking as much as possible in your shoes will also help your skin to harden. If in doubt, try another pair. If you have a pair of 'old favourites', be mindful that they need to last the better part of 300 miles, so do not take shoes that are too worn down and have little tread left as it will be difficult to get replacements once you set off.

Socks & Gaiters

A good sock can significantly add to your hiking comfort. Most modern trail socks are made of merino wool or polyester. Both fibres have outstanding properties regarding moisture wicking and temperature regulation. Thick socks, especially those with hidden seams, provide cushioning and help the shoe embrace your foot evenly, reducing rubbing and blisters. Though less stylish in a shoes-shorts combo and slightly warmer, socks that go (well) above your ankle collect less grit and grass seed, keep your legs cleaner, and provide better protection from the sun, stinging nettles, and tick bites.

Another way to keep out stones and grit are gaiters. Besides high gaiters for snow treks, there are also short and light ankle gaiters, specifically designed for hikers wearing shorts and low socks. The gaiters wrap around or stretch above your ankle and go over your shoes, protecting the gap between sock and shoe from unwanted entrants.

Compression socks can be of use especially to those who have issues with blood clots, oedema, and thrombosis. Compression socks come in different lengths, from knee-high, to thigh-high, to full tights. There are different compression gradients to assist circulation. Lower gradients are usually prescription free while higher gradients may require consultation. In any case, if you are aware of a condition and/or over 40 years old, it is advisable to consult with your doctor to determine whether or not compression socks are appropriate.

Backpacks

Just like shoes, an ill-fitting backpack can cause considerable pain, which could be in the form of chafing along straps or back aches from a restrictive fit. When deciding on which backpack to use for your Pennine Way adventure, there are a multitude of styles, capacities, and functionalities to consider. Here is a list of decision criteria to find a pack that is right for you:

Criteria	Comment
Size	<table><tr><th>Size</th><th>Torso [cm]</th><th>Torso [inch]</th></tr><tr><td>Extra Small</td><td>up to 40</td><td>up to 15 ½</td></tr><tr><td>Small</td><td>40 - 45</td><td>15 ½ - 17½</td></tr><tr><td>Medium</td><td>45 - 50</td><td>17½ - 19½</td></tr><tr><td>Large</td><td>50 and up</td><td>19½ and up</td></tr></table> These are commonly used sizes (learn how to measure your torso further below). Some packs also come in different hip sizes – measure at widest part. Apart from the (vertical) torso size, the design and cut varies on packs and shoulder straps, making them more or less comfortable for broad- or narrow-shouldered people. Compare and try different packs.
Capacity	If you plan on camping and carrying cooking equipment, typical packs used on the Pennine Way have capacities of 50-65 litres (all packing capacity is measured in litres based on the medium size). Small and large can vary by +/- 3 litres. While you want to choose the smallest capacity to save weight, you also need to fit in all of your gear. The right capacity for you depends on how bulky your big items are, i.e. tent, sleeping bag, and pad, and how much and which clothing you plan to bring. Packs allow some flexibility by raising the top lid or strapping a tent or foam pad on the outside. However, this may mean that weight is not optimally distributed. See section *'Pack & Adjust your Pack'* below for details.
Weight	As with most other gear, the weight of a backpack is closely linked to comfort and price. Thick, comfortable padding along shoulder straps and hip belts adds to the scale. However, keep in mind that you will be carrying this pack all day for a minimum of two weeks (dependent upon your itinerary), so increasing the weight by adding additional comfort may be worthwhile.

Gear

	The durability of materials also affects the pack's weight. Light packs usually have very thin shell materials that require more caution with handling. They may also be less water resistant than packs that are more rugged. This should not be a decision criterion however as you can attach a waterproof cover in the event of rain.
Padding	The padding of shoulder straps, hip belt, and backside of the pack is the essential factor for how you perceive the comfort of a pack, especially when filled with up to 18kg (40lbs). Using an ultra-light backpack saves extra weight, but make sure you are comfortable with the limited padding and potential rubbing/chafing when the pack is loaded and you are in normal hiking motion.
Adjustability	Most modern internal frame packs are very similar regarding their adjustability. Shoulder straps and hip belts can be adjusted in length; load lifter straps connect the pack's top to the shoulder straps and keep the weight balanced near your centre; sternum straps connect the shoulder straps across the chest to tighten the pack's fit and increase stability. Some packs have an adjustable suspension, meaning the entire shoulder harness system can be slid up and down to customize the pack to the exact torso length. Compression straps along the sides and front of the pack pull the weight close to your centre and keep contents from shifting on difficult trail sections. Daisy chains[4], elastic straps, or tool loops allow you to arrange and adjust gear on the outside of the pack.
Compartments	Having certain compartments may not be a key decision factor, however, having a well thought-out design can make trail days easier. Some hikers may

---

[4] A series of vertical loops of webbing for securing items to a backpack. Daisy chains are usually placed up along the center of the pack.

Gear

	insist on a sleeping bag compartment at the bottom of the pack, others may look for a certain number of side pockets to organise and access their content, and still others may want one or two water bottle pockets if that is their chosen hydration strategy. Having a multitude of compartments may facilitate pack organisation, however, it may also conflict with a minimalist, ultra-light approach.
Ventilation	A well-ventilated back area with airy padding is a big plus, especially on the Pennine Way in summer. Keep ventilation in mind when choosing a pack. It not only adds to your general comfort, but a dry back and shoulders are also less susceptive to chafing. Different brands and models have various approaches on how to wick moisture and heat from in-between your back and your pack. Some have air channels between padding, others completely separate the pack from the hiker's back with a tension mesh. Some ventilation methods are more effective and/or comfortable than others. Try them out to find the one that works best for you.
Hydration	A standard feature of most packs and worth asking about: a clip inside the pack to hang the hydration pack and an opening to lead the drinking tube to the front.
Frame	There are two frame styles: internal and external frames. Most modern backpacks have internal frames sewn into the pack. Traditionally, packs only had external frames with large aluminium tubes extending above and around the pack. Advantages of the external frame packs are low cost, light weight, and easy packability of bulky items (esp. on the outside). Disadvantages are their limited adjustability and fit, they are less stable on uneven terrain, and they are usually less water resistant.

	Internal packs make up for the above disadvantages, but are usually more expensive and heavier.
Rain cover	A built-in rain cover, usually located in the top lid or at the bottom of the pack, can be wrapped around the entire backpack with an elastic trimming. They are very practical, especially on the Pennine Way. If it does not come as a standard feature, consider acquiring a fitting cover for your pack separately.

Table 12 – Backpack Decision Criteria

Depending on your itinerary and preferred accommodation option, we would recommend the following capacity backpacks: Camping the entire way with all equipment included, you will need a large backpack of 50 litres or greater depending on the size of your gear. If you are walking between hostels and bunkhouses, whereby you don't need a tent but you do need to provide your own sleep gear (sleeping bag, sleeping pad, etc.), then a pack of 30-40 litres should be adequate. If you are hiking between B&Bs/hotels, just carrying your essentials for the day, then a 20-30 litre day pack should suffice.

Excursion – Measuring your torso length:

1. Locate your 7th cervical vertebra (C7) at the base of your neck by tilting your head forward. It is the bony bump at the end your vertical spine as your neck is leaning forward. When you run your fingers down your neck, you will first feel the smaller C6 and then C7. This marks the top of your torso.
2. Locate your iliac crest at the top of your hip bone by placing your hands high on your hips. With your thumbs in the back, dig into your pelvis to find the rounded, highest point of your hip bone. The imaginary line between your thumbs marks the bottom of your torso.
3. Measure between top and bottom of your torso. Be sure to stand straight. Assistance while handling the tape measure is helpful.

Pack & Adjust your Pack

As you pack your backpack, pay attention to two things: the weight distribution and the internal organisation of your gear.

Regarding weight distribution, it is important to keep heavy items close to your back and centred both vertically and horizontally (see Figure 8). Moderately heavy items should be placed around the heavy items, light ones along the perimeter of the pack (e.g., placing your sleeping bag in the bottom compartment). The goal is to bring the weight in the backpack as close to the centre of your back as possible. This way, the pack's centre of gravity is closest to your own, making it less likely for you to lose your balance.

A well-considered internal organization and distribution of gear among the compartments and pockets of your pack can save time and nerves. Gear that will only be used once at camp in the evening can be placed inside and below heavy items. Tent poles can also be separated from the tent bag for better storability. Depending on the specific partitioning of your pack, you will see during the first days of hiking, which compartments are best suited for what gear. Once sorted out, it then helps to stick to a specific organisation.

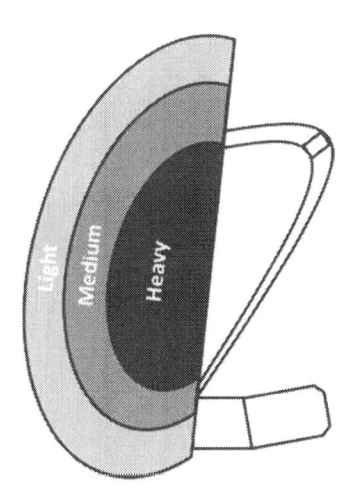

Figure 8 – Ideal Backpack Weight Distribution

For easier organisation in the main compartment, it is good to use thin plastic bags or (water-resistant) compression sacks. They can be individually stuffed and make accessing contents more convenient while providing additional protection against water and dirt. Valuables (e.g., phone, keys, money) can be kept in a zip lock bag and buried deep, as they will hardly be needed. Keep rain gear easily accessible (incl. large plastic bin bag if you do not have a rain cover). Once you have all your items in place and are ready to take off, pull all compression straps. They are usually located on the sides of your pack and at the top. Tightening the compression straps brings the weight closer to your back and inhibits gear from shifting.

ⓘ Anything that needs easy and frequent access, such as a map, sunscreen, snacks, or a pocket knife, should be stored in an accessible outside pocket near/on the top.

Adjusting your pack starts by putting it on correctly. If your pack is heavy, place one foot forward and lift the pack onto your thigh. Then, slip into the shoulder straps and lean forward, pulling the pack onto your back. As you lean forward, position the pack so the hip belt is centred comfortably over your hip bone, then close and tighten the hip belt firmly. As you straighten yourself up, your shoulder straps should be loose and 100 percent of the pack's weight on your hips. In this starting position the shoulder straps should have a gap of approximately 2.5 centimetres over your shoulders, however, the anchor points of the shoulder harness will be below your shoulders. If the straps already put pressure on your shoulders in the starting position and your pack has an adjustable suspension, slide the entire shoulder harness up a little and resecure it. Now, tighten your shoulder straps so they touch your shoulders.

Contrary to traditional backpacks, today's packs are supported primarily by the hip belt with only approximately 10 percent of the weight being carried by your shoulders. Keep this in mind as you adjust and tighten the straps. Then, pull your load lifters (that extend from the top of your shoulder straps to the top of your pack) so that they form a 45-degree angle to a horizontal. This brings the pack's centre of gravity closer to yours. Now, close your sternum strap and tighten comfortably in front of your chest. This reduces the pack's tendency of pulling your shoulders back. Finally, check your shoulder straps again. The shoulder straps should not be under great tension. Make sure you are merely guiding the weight, keeping it close to your centre of gravity, rather than carrying it with your shoulders.

Trekking Poles

Section 0d *Training* offered some advice on how to correctly use trekking poles. They can be of great service both for propulsion and providing a sense of security on steep stretches of the trail. Below is some advice on what to look out for when purchasing trekking poles:

- Good fit of grip and wrist strap: avoid sweaty grips (cork is favourable) and chafing straps
- The length of the pole should be easily adjustable
- The locking mechanism (twist or external lever) as well as the overall pole should be sturdy
- The lighter the pole, the better – lighter weight facilitates correct use and is less exhausting
- Shock absorbers can be useful, but are mostly a matter of taste – try them out
- Rubber tips absorb shock and muffle impact noise – more grip on rock, less on soft subsoil

c. Sleeping

Resting better enhances every aspect of your camping experience and is crucial if you're to enjoy your long-distance hike and have a productive next day. To ensure warmth, comfort, and dryness, which should be your main goals for a good night's sleep, you need an adequate sleeping system. Whilst for most hikers this will consist of a tent, sleeping bag, and sleep pad, there are some alternatives that you may wish to consider. A thrifty hiker can save a lot of money and weight by thoroughly planning their configuration. Having a flexible system also allows you to exchange individual items as and when the temperature and weather change, without having to purchase duplicate gear. This section supports your decisions in putting together a comfortable sleeping environment.

Shelters

If you are hiking as a couple, sharing a tent may be the most convenient and comfortable option. Should you be joined by a hiking buddy, the weight savings might be exceeded by the benefits of having separate sleeping arrangements. Figure 9 depicts the three most common shelter options:

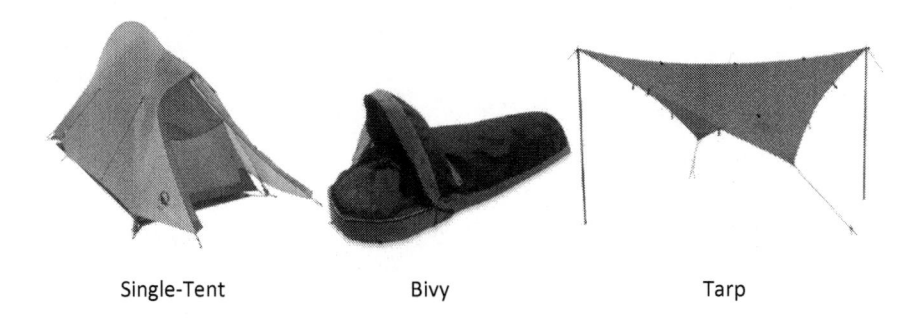

Single-Tent   Bivy   Tarp

Figure 9 – Sleeping Shelter Options[5]

Tent

A tent provides the most space for you to dress and move around inside as well as for keeping your gear sheltered. Remember, not only rain but also condensation, especially in close proximity to lakes and rivers, will settle overnight and can soak your gear. If it does happen to rain, is very windy, and/or you are cold, quickly pitching your tent and jumping inside provides instant protection and comfort. Getting food ready while taking a look at the map inside can be quite cosy, too. While the lightest single person tents are only around 1kg (2 lbs), carrying a tent is the heaviest option for shelter.

As tents are usually made of rather thin fabrics to keep down the weight, unless already included, adding a footprint to your setup might be a good

---

[5] Tent: Big Agnes, Bivy: Outdoor Research, Tarp: Kelty

idea. These durable, waterproof sheets are placed underneath the tent to protect the bottom from moisture and punctures.

Bivy

A bivouac sack, commonly known as 'bivy', is slightly bigger than a sleeping bag. The sleeping bag slides into the bivy, which is made of water- and wind-resistant material. A bivy sack has a small hole or breathable fabric in the head area which can either be left open or zipped shut. The head area generally also features a little dome, providing some extra space to rest on your elbows inside. While bivies offer similar insulation and protection from the elements as tents, inner condensation is a greater problem because fabrics get in direct contact with the sleeping bag, resulting in reduced air circulation. Also, bivies offer no additional space for gear or extensive movement, and people with claustrophobia may not appreciate the confined space.

Under the Stars/Tarp

To anyone counting grams, a tent or even bivy might sound like a lot to carry. An alternative widely discussed in forums is sleeping under the stars as the night sky is spectacular. However, as there is a very good chance it will rain at some point during your trip, using a tarp for camping in northern England is not recommended. Likewise, tarps will rarely be as good a wind deflector or as insulating as a tent or bivy. So if you do choose this alternative, make sure your sleeping bag is adequate to combat the temperatures including the wind-chill. A simple tarp may be the lightest and cheapest shelter but offers the least protection and privacy. It would definitely not suffice in persistent heavy rain, so you may find yourself seeking refuge in the nearest hotel or B&B!

On our trip, we used a two-person tunnel tent with a separate fly and inner, which offered us plenty of space as we were spending so much time in it. We appreciated the additional area of the porch, where we stored our packs at night. This also provided us with an undercover area to cook during wet weather. Although our choice of tent was relatively heavy compared with others, it was an item we had purchased previously, so we couldn't justify the upgrade costs of something more streamlined at that time.

Sleeping Bags

Sleeping bags come in an overwhelming multitude of varieties. It is all the more important to understand what the relevant features for this adventure are, whilst keeping in mind future possibilities, as a sleeping bag is a significant investment that should last for 15+ years.

Warmth, expressed by the bag's temperature rating, is your primary decision factor. Fortunately, there is a standardised warmth measurement that lets you easily compare[6]. Ratings are in the form of 'upper limit', 'comfort', lower limit', and 'extreme'. The 'comfort' rating refers to the optimum temperature you will feel warm and comfortable sleeping when in a relaxed position. When the bag is used in any temperatures below the 'comfort' rating, the user is likely to feel the cold. On average, women feel the cold more than men so this rating is some degrees above the 'comfort' limit for a man.

Depending on which month you are planning to hike the Pennine Way, choose a bag with a comfort zone temperature that is equal to or lower than the average low temperature of that month. For example, average daily lows in summer only drop to around 10°C (50°F), so where the weather is mild, a 1- to 2-season sleeping bag with a temperature rating of +5 degrees will be sufficient, although it is always better to opt for a lower comfort zone to be on the safe side. A 1-season sleeping bag is ideal for indoor use, for example when staying in a hostel.

When camping between late spring and early autumn, a 2-season bag is usually sufficient. However, as the UK weather and temperatures can be very erratic, for peace of mind we would recommend a 3-season sleeping bag for camping. This will have a comfort zone that is more than adequate,

---

[6] EN Standard 13537: A European Standard for the testing, rating, and labelling of sleeping bags.

and if you find you are getting too hot, you can always unzip your bag and use it as a quilt or even sleep on top of it should night time temperatures remain in double figures.

All peak performance sleeping bags use down insulation with fill-powers[7] of 700-900. Down is breathable and provides incredible loft and resulting insulation for its light weight while also compressing well. Additionally, there are new hydrophobic/dry downs that maintain insulation properties after getting wet and/or even repel moisture. Modern synthetic fill materials mimic the great properties of down, often at a very competitive price.

Weight is a general concern. Besides the filling, the weight is a function of length, girth, cut, fabric, and other features of the bag. Length of the bag is usually a pretty clear decision based on your height. Girth will primarily be determined by your shoulders and belly or hips. Cut refers to the bag's shape: most bags available today are mummy style, which follows the contours of the body – wider at the shoulders and narrow along legs and feet. Some bags are cut straight, providing more space but also more material to carry. Fabrics lining the sleeping bag are usually made of lightweight synthetic materials. Features include hoodies, draft tubes[8], zippers, inside pockets, and more. Take a look at different features and styles to find out if you care about any of them in particular. If not, cross them off your list of sleeping bag must-haves and save the weight.

Combining the above aspects leads to the warmth-to-weight ratio. This figure compares the bag's temperature rating to its weight. Best ratios are achieved with hood-less, no-frills, down mummy bags that have reduced padding in the back. However, going ultra-light requires some experience, especially on how to substitute certain weight savings on one piece of gear with another gear item that is already part of your essentials. If it requires adding another piece of gear that is non-essential, it defeats the purpose.

---

[7] Fill-power: a measure of the loft of a down product in cubic inches per ounce; it describes to what volume one ounce of down expands to.

[8] Draft tube: an insulating flap or tube that covers the zipper to avoid heat loss out of the sleeping bag.

For instance, the lack of an attached hood on a sleeping bag can be compensated with a hooded down jacket and/or a warm hat, which anyone will most likely pack anyway. The padding in the back, which is compressed when lying on it and, hence, loses its insulating properties, can be reduced if the sleeping pad offers sufficient insulation.

Pack size is another important factor. It is strongly correlated with the bag's warmth and weight – unfortunately, also with its price. Everything that reduces the weight usually reduces the pack size. In contrast, warmer bags with more filling typically do not compress as much. In this trade-off, do not opt for an inadequate comfort zone to reduce compression size unless you have a plan to make up for that loss of warmth.

Fit and feel should be agreeable to provide the most comfort. Materials should feel pleasant, and you should have sufficient space around your shoulders, hips, and feet based on your subjective preference. Some people find mummy sleeping bags to be confining, others feel suffocated by a draft collar, and still others prefer a snug fit. A good outdoor store should have several models for testing – try them and find out which type you are.

Lastly, choosing your sleeping bag must match your choice of camping strategy. If you are sleeping without a shelter, your sleeping bag should be particularly warm, wind- and water-resistant. However, water-resistant shells are less breathable and require more time for your bag to loft. If you plan to save weight on filling and frills by wearing a down jacket, make sure the sleeping bag provides enough inner space for the jacket's loft. In the end, deciding on a particular sleeping bag will be a compromise between choosing desired features and staying within a reasonable budget.

Taking all of these aspects into consideration, we chose an expensive, high quality down sleeping bag that has a comfort rating of -2°C (28°F). Our decision was not based purely on hiking in England. We wanted a bag that would be suitable for several of our planned trips, e.g., South America and the USA, so our final choice needed to meet several criteria. Again, it depends on your budget, but as we wanted a lightweight bag we avoided heavy synthetic materials which are generally cheaper to purchase. Our down sleeping bags were the perfect choice for us in terms of both temperature and comfort.

(i) A sleeping bag doesn't warm your body. It merely traps the heat your body produces to allow you to remain warmer. If your body is exhausted and unable to produce proper warmth, you will remain cold regardless of the bag rating. To ensure against this, eat a robust, fatty meal just before bed to fuel your thermogenesis. Your body will generate more heat breaking down the fat than it will carbohydrates or sugar. Also remember to keep hydrated as being dehydrated leads to lower heat production.

Something else you can do is to remember to loft early. When compressed, sleeping bags temporarily lose their insulation potential as the surface area for trapped air between the fibres / down plumes is reduced. Once it's out of the compression bag, air is drawn in, the bag expands and insulation potential is restored. As soon as you arrive at camp, set up your shelter and assemble your sleep system. Leave your bag to loft whilst you get on with other tasks such as preparing your evening meal.

Sleeping Pads

As well as a sleeping bag, don't forget the importance of a really good sleeping mat, which reduces heat loss through the ground, maximising your warmth, thereby supporting a good night's sleep. The two main criteria in your choice of sleeping pad are cushioning and insulation. Inflating and closed cell sleeping mats are most popular because of their comfort and weight. You can compare three equally suitable alternatives below:

Air Pads – Similar to the ones used in swimming pools, camping air pads have a thin air-tight shell that is inflated through a mouth valve. In order to cut down on weight, they are often semi-rectangular in shape. Air pads are very light-weight, roll-up very small, and offer exceptional cushioning, especially those with a thickness of 5 centimetres (2 inches) and up. On the downside, inflating a thick pad may require more than a minute of lung blasting, lightweight models can be noisy due to crackling material, and punctures are a concern. This type of pad is our preferred choice in terms of comfort, however, we have encountered several problems with regards to leaky valves, punctures, and chambers coming unstuck inside the pad, despite trying a couple of brands.

Foam Pads – Usually made of dense, closed-cell foams, foam pads can either be rolled up or folded like an accordion. Foam pads are light-weight, inexpensive, provide great insulation, and are practically indestructible from rough surfaces. On the downside, foam pads are usually not very thick and provide limited cushioning comfort. They also do not compress, hence packing rather large.

Self-inflating Foam Pads – Combining the packability of an air pad with the cushioning of a foam pad, while needing only little additional inflation. Thin pads are light-weight and compress well into a small sack. On the downside, they offer limited cushioning, while thicker pads of over 5 centimetres (2 inches) are very heavy.

ⓘ Whichever option you choose, make sure the pad is long enough and sufficiently wide at your shoulders. A good test is to lay on the pad in the shop before purchasing. If camping on the Pennine Way, a point to note is that your tent will generally be pitched on grass, so it should pose no threat to the integrity of your sleeping pad if you are concerned about it getting punctured.

Additional Comfort

Apart from the clothing you wear in your sleeping bag, there are other gear items that can provide additional comfort, such as a pillow, eye mask, ear plugs, and insect repellent.

ⓘ An alternative to packing an inflatable pillow is using your sleeping bag's stuff sack as a casing and stuffing it loosely with clothes.

An eye mask can be helpful to people with light-sensitive eyes, especially during a bright full moon or a very early sunrise. You could use your buff or scarf to make a blindfold by rolling it over your eyes – it might not seem comfortable at first, but it definitely does make a difference. Ear plugs can be tricky, but if you cannot get any sleep due to surrounding noises, they are useful. Insect repellent can also come in handy, especially when camping near water or you are without a shelter.

Lighting in the dark is also important to think about – for camp preparations in the evenings, early or late hiking, reading in the tent, and when nature calls at night. Headlamps are great because you have both hands free which is useful in any of the above scenarios (ensure adequate battery life). Another option are solar lamps, which come in an increasing variety. In any event, opt for energy-efficient LED light sources and remember to keep your light within reach at night.

d. Food & Water

Whilst Section 5b *Food* discussed options for meals, supporting itineraries that involve camp cooking or dining out or a mixture of both, this chapter focusses on various gear items needed to store, prepare, and consume food for cooking your own meals. It also provides information on how to treat and store water effectively.

Stove & Fuel

The preparation of your meals will undoubtedly require a stove as campfires are illegal on private land in England without the landowner's permission. They are also prohibited at many designated campsites, although they may be allowed if campers adhere to the stipulation of using a fire pit or BBQ grill, thereby keeping fires off the ground. Nevertheless, camping stoves are generally a much more convenient and efficient option when it comes to timely meal preparation, and are nowadays light and reliable, supporting the *Leave No Trace* ethic. There are two common stove fuel systems – gas canisters and liquid fuel – that are almost certainly in stock at the few camping supplies and outdoor gear shops situated at towns and villages close by the main route. (Although you may find that prices for these cooking essentials are inflated in the more remote areas.)

Gas Canisters

Gas canisters are filled with a pressurized gas mix of isobutane and propane. They have a self-sealing valve at the top and thread. Stoves can be screwed directly onto the tops. The thread securely connects the stove to the canister, using it as a stand. These stoves are extremely light (85g/<3oz) and pack very small.

Figure 10 – Canister Stove Options: Top-Mounted and Fuel Line

Stoves can also be connected remotely. These remote stoves are placed on the ground and connected to the canister via a fuel line. Consequently, the canister can be flipped on its head, also referred to as an inverted canister. Inverting the canister allows operation in liquid feed mode. This way, gas does not (need to) vaporise inside the canister. By avoiding the need for vaporisation, the gas can be used at lower (sub-evaporation) temperatures and performance is upheld. Especially in cold conditions, this comes in handy as the output is increased even with only little gas remaining. In addition, placing the stove directly on the ground can also improve pot stability and wind shielding.

The third pressurised gas setup is called an integrated canister system. These systems have an integrated burner and heat exchanger that are directly attached to the bottom of a pot for optimum heat transfer. The compact units are well shielded against wind, and their pots are often insulated against heat loss. Integrated canister systems are especially efficient for boiling water. However, it's in their nature that they cannot be remotely fed and, thus, have limited cold weather performance.

Generally, all canister systems are easy and fast to use as they do not require priming. They burn cleanly, reach their maximum heat very quickly, and there is no risk of fuel spillage. On the downside, pressurised gas is rather expensive and gauging how much fuel is left is difficult. Upright mounted canisters (not inverted) bear the risk of tipping over and struggle with the properties of gas, which lead to limited cold-weather operability and reduced performance as canisters empty.

Excursion – Operating pressurised gas canisters in cold weather – understanding the limits:

The lowest operating temperature of a pressurized gas canister is a matter of its gas composition. Good hiking canisters consist of isobutane and propane, large BBQ canisters often contain n-butane. A canister gas' operating temperature limit is determined by the gas with the highest (warmest) boiling point. Since propane has the lowest boiling point temperature (see Table 13), it will burn off first, especially in an upright canister system.

Boiling Point	**° Celsius**	**° Fahrenheit**	**Approx. Limit**
N-Butane	+/- 0	31	5°C (41°F)
Isobutane	-11	12	-6°C (21°F)
Propane	-42	-44	-37°C (-35°F)

Table 13 – Boiling Points of Stove Canister Gases at Sea Level

If only n-butane is left, the stove's working limit would be around 5°C (41°F), because the stove system needs a certain pressure to operate, which requires some thermal energy exceeding the respective boiling temperature to vaporise the gas. Otherwise, at lower temperatures, the n-butane would sit as a non-vaporising liquid at the bottom of the canister. This explains the positive effect of a remote liquid-fed stove and inverting the canister. The composition of the liquid gases remains constant, i.e., the gas that is less adequate for cold weather is not left behind to cause the canister to fade when approaching depletion.

A canister with a propane-isobutane mix would reach its limit around -6°C (21°F). However, as the air pressure drops with increasing altitude, so do the gases' boiling points. So as you ascend, your gas canister will be able to operate at lower temperatures than at sea level. A lapse rate for this effect is to subtract 1°C from the temperature limit for every 300 metres in elevation gain or 2°F for every 1,000 feet.

The excursion adds an important selection criterion: the gas composition. For summer trips on the Pennine Way, canister stoves are very well suited if they contain a propane-isobutane mix. With an operating temperature limit of -6°C (21°F) at sea level and approx. -16°C (1°F) at 3,000 metres (10,000 ft.) elevation, they will provide reliable heat along the trail. Liquid feed canister stoves offer additional low temperature range.

> [!] Remember, the fuel temperature is key, not the ambient temperature. When confronted with very cold conditions, keep your canister inside your tent or even at your feet in the sleeping bag to ensure the gas temperature is a few degrees above its boiling point.

Liquid Fuel

Liquid fuel stoves have a similar setup as remote liquid-fed canister systems. The burner is placed on the ground and connects via a fuel line to the bottle fuel tank, which has a pump to pressurise the fuel and a valve to control flow. Most systems require priming, especially in cold conditions. Priming means that a few drops of fuel are placed into a dish underneath the burner and lit. This heats the attached fuel line and causes the fuel to vaporise and push into the actual burner where it can be ignited.

Figure 11 – Liquid Fuel Stove

Liquid fuel systems are dominated by white gas (a.k.a. naphtha). This is a highly refined fuel with little impurities so it burns very clean. There are also multi-fuel stoves that run on white gas, kerosene, diesel, and gasoline. Generally, the greatest advantages of a (petroleum-based) liquid fuel stove are the easy international availability of its fuels, their low cost, very high heat output, and their ability to operate at low temperatures. White gas, for example, freezes at -30°C (-22°F) to which the stove is operable. Downsides are that some fuels are odorous, smoke, and may blacken pots. The stoves, especially multi-fuel models, are rather expensive. Flames are not as finely adjustable for simmering foods and overall operation (incl. pumping and priming) needs some practice and bears the risk of flares or burns. Stoves require regular maintenance to avoid clogging, even more so the less purified the fuel is. All this requires some experience and commitment.

Regarding weight, liquid fuel systems are heavier than canisters, due to the more complex burner and pump-valve system for the bottle tanks. Additionally, petroleum fuels have an approximately. 5 percent lower energy density than commonly used pressurised gases. However, liquid fuel tanks are reusable and can be filled as needed, whereas gas canisters can only be bought in a few sizes, making incremental adjustments to fuel supplies difficult.

Fuel Calculation

This leads to the very important question of how much fuel to carry. Unless your meal plan requires special preparation, your fuel consumption will be in direct proportion to how much water you will be boiling per day. A good approximation of how much fuel is needed to boil water is 11.5 grams of fuel per litre of water or 0.012 ounces of fuel per ounce of water. If certain meals require simmering after the water has boiled, add 1 gram (0.035 oz.) of fuel per minute of cooking time.

Figure 12 shows the equation used to estimate fuel consumption per trail section, i.e., days until resupply. Remember to consider all your sections, including side trips, and think about which fuel tank sizes or gas canisters are best suited to provide sufficient energy while minimising weight.

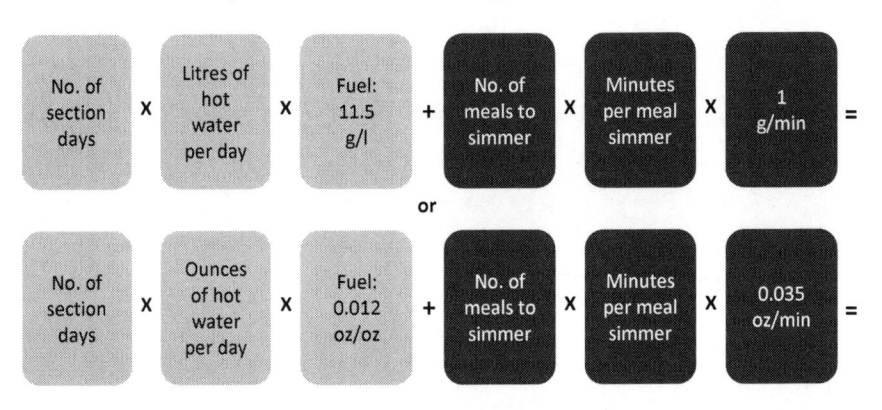

No. of section days × Litres of hot water per day × Fuel: 11.5 g/l + No. of meals to simmer × Minutes per meal simmer × 1 g/min =

or

No. of section days × Ounces of hot water per day × Fuel: 0.012 oz/oz + No. of meals to simmer × Minutes per meal simmer × 0.035 oz/min =

Figure 12 – Estimating Fuel Needs

One example for estimating fuel consumption:

Anna is planning 15 days on the Pennine Way with one resupply after 8 days; i.e., her first section is 8 days and her second section is 7 days long. Her estimates for hot water demand per day are as follows:

	235ml (8oz)	for coffee in the morning
+	235ml (8oz)	for porridge/oatmeal
+	0ml (0oz)	for lunch
+	470ml (16oz)	for a meal in the evening
+	235ml (8oz)	for one cup of tea
=	1.2l (40oz)	of boiling water per day

Five of her meals on the first section each have to be simmered for ten minutes. The rest of them are dehydrated/instant meals that do not require simmering. Consequently, her fuel estimates for section one (S1) and two (S2) are as follows:

In Grams:

S1: (8 x 1.2l x 11.5g/l) + (5 x 10min x 1g/min) = 160g

S2: (7 x 1.2l x 11.5g/l) + 0 = 97g

In Ounces:

S1: (8 x 40oz x 0.012oz/oz) + (5 x 10min x 0.035oz/min) = 5.6oz

S2: (7 x 40oz x 0.012oz/oz) + 0 = 3.4oz

In total, Anna needs approximately 257 grams (9 oz.) of fuel for the entire trip. Consequently, she could opt to take only one 227 grams (8 oz.) canister of fuel, gross weight 374 grams (13.1 oz.), for the entire trip by reducing her hot water demand a little. Otherwise, she will either have to carry a larger/second canister with her or purchase extra fuel along the way.

ⓘ In order to keep boiling times and wasted fuel low, always use a lid, start on a small flame, and increase as water gets warmer, never turning to full throttle. Furthermore, use a windscreen or heat reflector around your stove and pot to shield against your greatest enemy while cooking.

Lastly, do not forget to bring proper means to ignite a flame. Options include gas lighters, matches, piezo igniters, and spark strikers. Opt for something that is durable, long-lasting, reliable, and water-resistant. It is not recommended to solely rely on one option. Bring at least one redundant option as a backup in case your first choice gets wet or breaks.

Pots, Pans and Utensils

Deciding which kind of pot and/or pan to bring depends on your choice of food and on the amount of people you will be cooking for. For example, if you are cooking for 1-2 people, one pot with a capacity of approximately 1

Gear

litre/34 ounces is sufficient. The more liquid the contents are, i.e., soups or water, the better the heat energy circulation and the narrower the pot's base can be. Especially, if you plan on only boiling water during a summer trip, an integrated canister system is the quickest and most efficient way of heating. However, if you intend to prepare solid meals, opt for a pot or pan with a wider base. Especially then, choose an easy-to-clean, non-stick surface.

In either case, materials such as aluminium or titanium help save pack weight and always using a lid conserves your fuel. Whether the pot or pan has an integrated (foldable) handle or comes with a multi-use detachable one is secondary. A more important feature is how well pots and dishes can be stored inside each other whilst not in use.

While putting together your meals, it helps to think about and set aside the utensils it will take to prepare them. The standard minimum is usually a spoon or 'spork' (spoon and fork in one) and a pocket knife. Extra-long plastic spoons are particularly convenient when eating directly out of freeze-dried meal pouches or the pot. However, if your meals require stirring or flipping on the stove, make sure your utensil is heat resistant.

Water Treatment

As discussed earlier in the book, it is advised to treat any water from natural sources before drinking. There are six options for doing so: micro-filter pumps, micro-filter gravity and squeeze bags, ultra-violet (UV) sterilization pens, chemical tablets/drops, and boiling. Table 14 provides an overview of respective capabilities, features, and costs. Similar to other gear items, choosing an appropriate water treatment system is a trade-off. Below is a summary of the key takeaways from the overview table to aid decision-making:

- Pump filters are fast and work well even in little, murky water, but they are rather heavy and require some maintenance.
- Gravity filters are fast, very easy to use, and the clean tank can double as a hydration pack, but they are expensive and rather heavy.
- Squeeze filters are fast, light, cheap, and filter large amounts of water per cartridge (life span of over 10,000l/cartridge), but the squeezing is strenuous and the pouch can easily tear or puncture if squeezed too hard.
- UV lights often come as a pen or integrated in a bottle. They are light, rather fast, and treat viruses, but they rely on batteries to work and somewhat clear water to be effective.
- Chemical options are chlorine dioxide, sodium dichloroisocyanurate, and iodine tablets or droplets. They are very light, cheap, and treat viruses, but slower than other options and less effective in murky water. Plus, a slight chemical aftertaste usually remains. Also, the individual tablet dosage should match your drinking container size. Some tablets are for two litres of water and hard to break. In case your container has a different volume, droplets are an alternative.
- Boiling water can only be a backup option. It is slow, heavy (incl. the fuel needed), and leaves you with hot water to quench your thirst on a hot afternoon.

Generally, filters treat protozoa, bacteria, and particles, and allow instant water consumption. Boiling, UV light, and chemical purifiers are effective against protozoa, bacteria, and viruses, however, only if the drawn water is almost clear and after a certain treatment time. All options except pumps are of limited applicability in shallow or small amounts of water.

Feature	Boiling	Chemical	UV Light	Squeeze	Gravity	Pump
Speed [l/min]	0.2	0.1-0.25	0.7-1.0	1.5-1.7	1.4-1.8	1.0-1.6
Weight [g]	10/l	50-80	120-170	60-150	230-340	280-420
Treats Viruses	yes	yes	yes	no	no	no
Longevity [l]	n/a	80-100	>10k	>10k	1-2k	1-2k
Ease of Use	easy	very easy	easy	medium	very easy	easy
Durability	long	n/a	fair/long	fair	long	fair/long
Cost [£]	25-35 p/l	5-10 p/l	50-100	20-35	50-80	50-65
Comment	Requires fuel and drinking hot water	Ineffective in murky water; virus treatment, but >0.5h, slight chemical taste	Ineffective in murky water, requires batteries/ charging	Hard squeezing led to pouch tears, hand strength needed	Best if hung, incl. storage bags, great for groups	Pre-filter filters large particles, requires maintenance

Table 14 – Water Treatment Options

Water Storage

It is also worth putting some thought into how to store the treated water for convenient and frequent access. Choosing the right water storage and hydration system is a matter of personal preference and hiking strategy. Two options are most common – water bottles and hydration packs.

Practical bottle sizes are 0.75-1.5 litres (24-48 oz.). Aluminium, stainless steel, and BPA-free plastic are the most used and suitable materials. Features like narrow or wide openings, sealing valves, and straws are up to personal preference. Insulated bottles are also available but are generally heavier and have less capacity. Bottles with loops allow attaching to the backpack with a karabiner.

Hydration packs consist of a reservoir made of puncture-resistant, durable material that is placed inside your backpack and a connected drinking tube through which fluids are consumed. A bite valve at the end of the drinking tube helps control the flow of the fluid. The tube can be clipped onto your backpack strap or lapel for easy access when not in use. Typical sizes of reservoirs are 2-3 litres (65-100 oz.). Wide openings ease filling and cleaning of hydration packs. Built-in loops at the top allow hanging of the reservoir inside the backpack.

ⓘ Before hiking: if your hydration pack has a plastic taste, mix a few tablespoons of baking soda, 1 litre (32 oz.) of warm water, and some clear vinegar, and let it soak in the reservoir over night; then rinse thoroughly.

ⓘ After hiking: clean well and keep reservoir open and as expanded as possible during storage for air circulation, or store the dry pack in the freezer.

This leads to the question of what size your container(s) should be and how much water to carry each day. A non-scientific answer is to always carry approximately two litres. If you are very weight conscious, you can hike with half that amount on the Pennine Way, but you will need to look at the trail sections ahead of you and plan accordingly with where you are going to re-fill. Keep in mind that the more frequently you plan to resupply, the more often you will have to unpack your treatment gear. Also remember that some sections on the Pennine Way may be dry, causing a real difficulty with finding water in the hot summer months if you do not divert to villages or towns.

(i) In addition to your hydration pack/bottles, you may also want to bring a small one litre backup pouch/bottle to carry extra water for cooking during the last stretch of the day while looking for a camp site or simply as an emergency canister.

For completeness sake, do not forget to pack a cup/mug for drinking tea or coffee at camp. A common 500ml (17 oz.) plastic mug with a 'sippy' lid works great to limit spills and keep contents warm. It also doubles nicely as a measuring cup for food preparation.

e. Medical & Personal Care

For light-weight enthusiasts, this section may be particularly painful. It deals with bringing several items of which you hope never to use any. Nevertheless, a well-equipped first aid kit is vital in case of emergency. Your personal kit should include any medications you regularly take, including those that were recommended by your doctor for this specific trip. There are various well-equipped pre-packed first aid kits, however, hikers tend to have different needs and standards regarding personal care when outdoors. Limit yourself to the minimum you feel comfortable with. Below are some suggestions on what to pack:

First Aid – General

- Self-adhesive bandages
- Tape (sufficient for emergency and blisters)
- Antibacterial wipes/ointments
- Non-stick sterile pads
- Self-adhering elastic bandage wrap
- Scissors or knife (switchblade knives are illegal in the UK!)

- Pain relieving gels/creams (with Camphor, Menthol, Arnica)
- Anti-inflammatories and/or pain relievers (e.g., ibuprofen)
- Blister treatment (bandages, pads, etc.)
- Survival blanket (silver/insulated)
- Whistle

First Aid – Specific or Optional

- Any personal medication
- Anti-histamines (to remedy allergic reactions)
- Tweezers (for splinters and tick removal)
- Safety pins
- Insect-sting relief
- Sun relief (e.g., Aloe Vera)
- Blood thinner (e.g., Aspirin)
- Muscle sprain cream/gel
- Knee support

Personal Care

- Sunscreen (SPF 30 and up)
- Lip balm (with SPF)
- Tooth brush & paste
- Soap (biodegradable)
- Deodorant
- Insect repellent (suitable for midges)
- Moisturiser (sun cream can double up as this)

f. Other Essentials

To the reader, the following gear items can be just as important as the ones listed previously. Many choices are purely subject to personal preference. When deciding what other necessary items you are going to bring, remember that on a long-distance walk space is at a premium, and that the main bulk of your pack's weight should be kept to 'essential' items.

Gear	Comments
Camera	Consider the trade-off between weight and photo quality when deciding between SLR, compact, and smartphone cameras. Ensure you have enough batteries/memory cards to meet the needs of your itinerary. On the Pennine Way, you will find that charging is usually available at most types of accommodation, including some campsites.
Compass	Good to have, especially, when visibility is low.
GPS Watch	GPS watches, as used for running, show you exact distances travelled, speed, pace, elevation, etc. Software allows you to trace your every step back home at the computer and import data into online maps. They are good to have, but not essential for navigating.
Map	As it is a *National Trail*, several maps are available to purchase showing the Pennine Way route, but the two most well-known are the Ordnance Survey Maps and the Harvey Maps series. Both options are discussed in more detail in Section 3a *Trails & Navigation*.
Map App	Having a printed map is highly advisable, even if you plan on using an app. There are several map apps for Android and iOS, so check for recent releases. With your phone's GPS, the app can precisely locate your position on the trail. Some give additional information, e.g., elevation profile.
Money	Bring cash to pay for campsites, food, drinks, stove gas, post cards, emergency, etc. Towns and larger villages have ATMs, where you can withdraw cash en route. Some smaller villages offer a cashback service at the local shop or post office.

Rope	Useful to hang clothes, replace a strap on a backpack, or as a shoe lace. It should not be too thick or heavy. 5m (16 ft.) is a good length. E.g., paracord, dyneema cord.
Shovel (optional)	Useful to bury human waste. Should be light but sturdy as the ground can be rocky and tough. A walking pole can double up for this function. Public conveniences are often available along the way.
Solar Charger (optional)	Very much dependent on how many electronic devices you are intending to carry and where you are intending to sleep. A variety of compact photovoltaic panels incl. rechargeable battery and (USB) power port are available. Make sure you have enough power if you plan to carry several devices (light, smartphone, watch, etc.).
Sunglasses	Sporty, tight fit, UV protection, polarisation is a plus.
Pack of Tissues	Keep a small pack of tissues, a small bottle of hand sanitiser and a small pack of wet wipes in your top lid for emergencies.
Towel	Quick drying, synthetic fabric, lightweight.
Sewing Kit & Duct Tape	Make sure your kit contains essentials for outdoor repairs, e.g., heavy duty thread, strong needle. (Safety pins and small scissors will already form part of your first aid kit.) Or bring one large eyed needle to easily thread dental floss, so it can have a dual purpose. Alternatively, duct tape fixes almost anything! Wrap some around your trekking poles for an emergency repair.

Table 15 – Other Essential Gear

Gear

7. Personal Experience

In this chapter, we describe our personal preparations, travel arrangements, gear items, and experiences on the Pennine Way. It is a summary of considerations and efforts that went into our 24-day trip in June/July 2014 and exemplifies what worked for us hiking as a couple. If you are inexperienced and/or unsure about certain options, we hope this gives you some additional reference points and guidance. We can honestly say this amazing journey on foot along the Pennines of England is one of the best walks we have ever done! Every day surprised us with its sense of wilderness yet accessibility, its toughness but sheer beauty. Hopefully, you'll be as inspired as us and have your own experiences to share after embarking on a Pennine Way adventure of your own!

a. Plan

Logistics

At the initial stages, we researched what a Pennine Way thru-hike would entail and read several blogs detailing other hiker's day-to-day experiences. Drawing knowledge from other people's first-hand experiences on the trail is an invaluable tool to get straight to the heart of whether the trail is for you or not. Then, we put together an achievable itinerary. After our initial research, we had already decided that we'd walk it in the traditional direction from south to north as Edale was easily accessible, being close to where we live in the Midlands. So we set about breaking the route up into manageable walking distances and making notes about good places to camp. We typed all of this information (which included daily mileage, campsite addresses, contact numbers and prices) into a spreadsheet, which we could access in our cloud drive on our smartphones. We also carried a paper copy as a backup.

Being born and bred in England, we knew what to expect in terms of the weather so this just ensured we had the most appropriate, light-weight kit suitable for all eventualities. (We hoped!)

As we were still on a career break, it was possible to start our hike in late June. We deliberately chose this month as it meant we could take advantage of the most hours of daylight, and, fingers crossed, the best of the weather, whilst avoiding the higher temperatures that can be reached during the height of summer. We also thought it would be prudent to avoid the peak time of July/August when in England families head to the countryside during the six-week school summer holidays.

We didn't book any lodgings in advance so that our itinerary was completely flexible, simply turning up at campsites on the day, seeking somewhere to pitch our tent. Transport was the only thing we had organised prior to leaving home. Knowing there is a regular service to Edale, connecting via Manchester or Sheffield, we booked our train tickets just a week beforehand. In expectation of completing the trail and arriving in Kirk Yetholm, we had also looked at various transport options for returning home.

Even though we considered ourselves reasonably fit and had a good amount of experience hiking in different parts of the world, we had never tackled a long-distance hike of this magnitude. So to ensure a greater chance of success, we devised a training schedule that involved day walks of around 10 miles in and around our local area, gradually building up to between 15 and 20 miles of walking per day. To help our bodies become accustomed to carrying our new 58-litre packs and cope with the increased weight, and so that our feet would harden and bed in our new trail shoes, we tried to walk at least three times a week, with at least one rest day in-between walks. Regular training also meant we had sufficient time to test our gear in different weather conditions and in terms of performance, durability, and comfort, and make adjustments if necessary.

Food & Resupply

Besides gear, if your itinerary involves camping and cooking your own meals, then food and nutrition will also play a major role in your planning and preparation. In addition to the suggestions in Section 5b *Food*, here are some personal remarks on the food we brought.

In general, we like to carry enough food to keep us going for two to three days, as well as a set of emergency rations kept at the bottom of our packs. This always ensures that we have adequate provisions should the location of shops be particularly sparse along certain sections of the route or if our intended arrival time does not coincide with opening hours. As stated previously, it is not really necessary to carry several days' worth of food with you or send yourself resupply packages as you can resupply almost daily along the way. We always advocate buying locally as this supports the community. Your custom is particularly important to the small local businesses that struggle to survive in remote rural areas.

Meal	Comments on our Food
Breakfast	Our standard breakfast was an individual sachet of porridge, made with boiling water and mixed with milk powder. (If we had a particularly long/intensive day ahead, then we would fill ourselves up with 2 sachets each and have 'double porridge'!) Our favourite breakfast meal was eggs – either fried in a cob, scrambled, or as an omelette with the addition of tomato, onion and cheese (if we had any). A cooked breakfast means more washing up and also takes longer to prepare, so it depended on how much time we had available before setting off. If we were in a rush, we would eat a granola bar at camp, then stop after an hour or so on the trail for a proper breakfast.
Lunch	Lunch depended on what we could purchase in various villages. If there was a larger Co-op supermarket, our preference was tortilla wraps with hummus or sandwich squares (square cobs) with cheese spread triangles. If we were limited on choice, we would have snacks, such as a pork pie, pasty, and sausage roll, as well as packets of crisps, crackers, peanuts, pretzels, or biscuits.
Snacks	We always carried a big bag of sweets and had at least one chocolate bar per day. We also bought granola snack bars and bags of mixed nuts/dried fruit. If fresh fruit was

	available, we would often buy an apple or punnet of plums.
Dinner	Dinner could be anything quick and simple, such as instant noodles or mashed potato, where we just added boiling water, to something much tastier like chicken curry, rice, and naan bread if we could get fresh ingredients like chicken breast. We adapted and experimented with meals depending on what food was available. We particularly liked burgers or sausage baps, making frequent use of our frying pan. One thing to have in mind is that whenever you are cooking fresh as opposed to just adding boiling water, cooking times are much longer so you will use up more gas. It is always good to carry an extra gas canister (mini) somewhere in your pack in case of emergency.
Condiments	We had salt, pepper, and spices, such as chilli and curry powder, mixed herbs, two mini bottles of olive oil, and various sachets of tomato sauce, brown sauce, and mayonnaise (that we had procured from eateries wherever they were available!), and we used them all. You may consider these items a luxury, but they really helped to make the food we were eating flavoursome and appealing. (After all, if you are eating noodles every day, you will soon get bored of them without a little variety!)

Table 16 – Overview of Personal Food & Comments

Our food rations and meal ideas worked well and suited us, not least because Wayne is a really good cook and can turn anything remotely 'instant' into something mouth-wateringly good. We both had defined camp roles – Wayne being the 'chef' and I being the 'washer-upper'. When we set up camp, I would always sort out the bedding and sleep gear, while Wayne got to work preparing dinner. I would not have welcomed the prospect of doing all of these tasks myself had I been hiking without a partner to share the roles and responsibilities. So if you have not got a

Personal Experience

hiking buddy, carefully consider whether you would rather put your feet up with a pint and have your dinner served to you in a pub or restaurant after a tiring days' walking, as opposed to cooking for yourself (and then having to wash your own dishes, too).

Gear

Our general attitude to gear is that 'you get what you pay for', so if you want gear of good quality that will stand the test of time, it is worth investing in and spending that little bit more. If you are hiking over a long distance, then the weight you are carrying is of significant importance. Light-weight gear options are therefore preferable, but these tend to be more expensive, so your budget will determine how lightweight you can actually go. A thorough scrutinising of your intended kit list is a good idea so that you can try and reduce your pack weight by discarding any unnecessary items.

We already owned most of the basic gear items as we often went on weekend hiking and camping trips. However, our original backpacks, tent, and sleeping bags were not purchased with thru-hiking in mind and were all heavy, bulky, and very much budget items bought on impulse. To help us achieve our goal, we decided to upgrade our kit and purchase new, lighter weight options that would better suit the trail and weather conditions as well as providing more comfort and reliability.

We anticipated the UK weather to be changeable and generally expected rain even though we were hiking in early summer, so we planned our gear accordingly. Below is an overview of our equipment along with some comments:

Gear	Comments
Backpack	Our backpacks are very light whilst still being capable of carrying a decent load due to a lightweight aluminium frame. The 'medium' sized 58-litre pack weighed approximately 1kg (2 lbs.). Side pockets, front

	pouch, and removable top lid provided easy access for all of our essentials. A point to note: Wayne was measured in-store and recommended the 'large' size pack, which is slightly bigger in dimensions with a volume of 61 litres, weighing 1.1kg. By the end of the summer, however, as he had lost about 9kg (20 lbs.) in weight, Wayne was finding that the hip belt was a little loose and could not be tightened any further. In hindsight, he should have opted to purchase the medium size pack.
Tent	Two-person tent, not particularly light at 2.5kg (5.5 lbs.), but the tent's redeeming qualities were the available space it provides and its double skin design. We decided to go with this option purely based on the fact that we thought it would be more suitable/reliable in heavy rain. What we liked particularly was the generously sized porch area that we used for storing both our backpacks, whilst still leaving room for cooking food or drying gear. The double skin and high hydrostatic head[9] of 4000mm also served us well in the aforementioned heavy rain. We modified the tent slightly by changing the guy lines for lighter ones and by investing in a lighter set of pegs, which shaved nearly 500g (1 lb.) off the total weight.
Sleeping bag	The sleeping bag we used is lightweight (about 850g) with a comfort zone down to freezing, featuring hydrophobic European goose down with an 800 fill power. It's made with Pertex Quantum GL inner and outer fabrics, a superlight material which allows the down to quickly and efficiently reach its maximum loft. It has a tapered mummy shape and half-length zip to allow for venting. It also comes with a roll-top waterproof compression stuff sack.

---

[9] Hydrostatic head is the measure of how water resistant the tent material is. It measures how tall a column of water the fabric can hold, before water starts to seep through the weave.

Personal Experience

	We found that these bags were more than adequate for the UK summer climate. In addition, we both use silk sleep liners, which tend to add an extra degree or two of warmth and comfort to your sleeping bag.
Sleeping pad	We used lightweight inflatable sleeping pads, which have since been discontinued due to persistent problems with leaky valves and punctures. However, we found them to be really comfortable and always had a great night's sleep when using them. One of the features we really liked about the mats was the larger outer tube that kept you from rolling off the side in your sleep. These when rolled up, were small and only weighed about 400 grams (<1 lb.).
Cook set, stove & utensils	We used a camping stove in combination with a compact cook set. The two-person cook set included two bowls, two cups, cooking pot with lid and space for your burner and small gas canister. We added a kitchen set, which included fold-away spoon, tongues and frying pan spatula, mini spice rack, and a small non-stick frying pan. You have more choice and variety on the Pennine Way as you can shop at local stores to get fresh ingredients. The mini frying pan, for example, was perfect for frying eggs in the morning for breakfast. In addition, our utensils consisted of two sporks, a pot stand, an outdoor knife (for cutting stuff up), and a long metal spoon (for stirring stuff in a tall pot). You might feel like we went a little overboard, however, we were really pleased with our additions to improve the quality and our enjoyment of food on the go.
Fuel	We used general propane/butane mix canisters with a screw on connector. These are usually available at outdoor gear/hardware shops, several campsites and some garages/petrol stations along the way.

Lighting device	We each carried and used a standard lighter, which were both reliable. We also carried windproof matches as a backup.
Water treatment	As clean and safe drinking water is readily available at your lodging, you may not consider hiking with any water treatment options. We do however fully recommend always carrying some water purification tablets with you for emergencies. As we planned on wild camping to break up the last section between Byrness and Kirk Yetholm, we also decided to carry a water filter with us for filtering water from rivers. We used a squeeze filter system that comprises of a filter unit, squeeze pouch, and small syringe for cleaning. You fill the pouch with water, attach to the filter, and squeeze the water through into your bottle.
Hydration pack	We didn't carry a hydration pack. Having previously used them in South America, we found them cumbersome in our backpacks. (Mine even split inside my pack soaking the contents. Luckily, most of my gear was protected in dry bags.) So instead, we decided to each carry two standard one litre water bottles that we filtered clean water into if we didn't have access to a tap (e.g., when wild camping). Should we need extra water, each of us carried a one litre squeeze pouch that we could fill in addition to our bottles.
Pocket knife	Lightweight outdoor knife, which doubled up as our chopping knife when cooking. *Note:* Switchblade knives are illegal in the UK!
First aid kit	An essential piece of our gear. It's not going to repair a broken leg or severed arm, but it will allow us to treat minor wounds when and if we get them. It is comprised of various plasters, sterile wipes, various dressings, medical tape, and blister plasters to which we've added some painkillers, anti-diarrhoea tablets, tick tweezers, antiseptic cream, and a small pack of

Personal Experience

	tissues. We always take this first aid kit with us and regularly check its contents and keep it topped up. We also carry small tubes of cold gel and pain relief rub to treat any aches and pains after a days' walking.
Silver survival blanket	This is always a useful safety item to carry should you ever need it. We have a standard silver survival blanket stowed in the bottom of our packs in case of emergency.
Sunscreen	SPF 30+. Bring a good supply, although it is possible to purchase in village pharmacies and supermarkets along the route.
Soap	We carried travel sized bottles of shower gel in 75ml quantities. (Depends on what you're willing to carry and your personal preference – a simple bar of soap does the job!)
Camera	Being keen photographers, cameras are an essential part of our kit. (Wayne would rather cut down on clothing & other personal items to allow himself more weight and space in his pack for camera gear!) Wayne: Compact system camera with 9-18mm & 25mm lens, plus tripod. Danielle: Point-and-shoot travel camera.
Map and/or map app	To navigate, we used the Harvey Pennine Way strip maps (south, central and north), which are a nice, compact size and the format is easy to follow. In addition, we used the ViewRanger app for android smartphone loaded with OS map set.
Money	We carried about £100 cash, topping up at ATMs if needed along the way. It is good to have cash to pay for campsites, cafes, small items, etc. However, most shops, restaurants, pubs, B&Bs, and hotels accept debit cards as a form of payment.

Rope	5m length of dyneema line, used mostly for hanging washing out to dry. (Walking poles doubled up as supports).
Shovel	None. We used out trekking poles to dig holes if needed.
Sunglasses	Ordinary, inexpensive UV-protection sunglasses.
Toilet paper	We always carry a small pack of tissues, small pack of wet wipes and a small bottle of hand sanitiser in our top lids for easy access.
Towel	Compact microfibre travel towels (120cm x 60cm) – one each.
Solar charger & LED lamp	We added a couple of gadgets to our kit to help keep our phones and cameras charged on the go. The first item is a battery pack. With its 13000mAh capacity, it has the juice to recharge a smart phone over six times. It has dual USB outputs (1A and 2A) and can charge smartphones as well as compact cameras. In addition, we used a solar panel to charge the battery pack above, Wayne's camera batteries (via the 12V output), and to keep his phone juiced when using the map app to record our GPS route.
Trekking poles	Lightweight carbon poles (390g/pair). We consider trekking poles to be an essential piece of kit, particularly if you're carrying a large load.

Table 17 – Overview of Personal Gear and Comments

For some, ultralight backpacking is the key to a successful thru-hike. For us, it is a balance between weight versus comfort, whilst having gear that is both reliable and durable. Sometimes compromises may have to be made due to budget limitations, but we believe items such as sleep system, footwear, and waterproof layers are always worth spending that bit extra on. Having purchased cheaper items in the past that literally fell apart on us after only wearing them a handful of times, then having to spend more money on replacing them, we can say without hesitation that gear that will stand the test of time is always worth investing in, so make your choices wisely!

b. Go

Day 1 – Edale to Kinder Scout (5.1 miles) – 'Wild at Heart'

Our Pennine Way adventure began with a train journey to the small Peak District village of Edale. From here, we intended to hike 16 miles to our first campsite at Crowden. However, in typical English style, it was raining when we arrived. So instead of setting off and getting soaked right away, we headed to the Old Nags Head Pub, our best alternative. We ordered ourselves a pint, as is customary to begin the Pennine Way, and mulled over the situation.

Figure 13 – Start of the Adventure and Old Nags Head Pub

So there we were debating whether to camp at the nearby Coopers Farm, stay in the pub and have a session, or just go for it and set off on the trail. We had a recce outside decided on the latter as the rain had almost stopped. So at 4.30 PM, we finally set off just as the sun made an impromptu appearance. Since setting off so late, we headed to the Kinder Plateau and decided that we would wild camp for the night. But first, we needed to refill our water bottles. We had no luck with streams as those we passed were dry but managed to find a trickle of water at Kinder Downfall. It was around 9:00 PM when we found a nice flat spot to pitch our tent past Kinder Downfall, above a place known as Sandy Heyes, which, incredibly, was our first wild camp spot in the UK!

Figure 14 – Jacob's Ladder and Wild Camping on Kinder

After a camp dinner, we settled in for the night. It was not to be a night of contented sleep. Far from it! I was still awake at 2:00 AM because I was so cold. We had made the last minute decision to bring our 2-season sleeping bags, thinking our 3-season down bags would be too hot for summer in the UK. Big mistake! Although Wayne was not quite as cold as I was, I had to put on all the layers I had. And still I could not get warm, which meant a restless night shivering away, until I finally nodded off as the sun came up.

Day 2 – Kinder Plateau to Crowden (10.9 miles) – 'Support Team to The Rescue'

Hardly any sleep during the night meant we did not make our 6:00 AM alarm call. In fact, we did not wake up until 8:00 AM, causing us to panic as we had planned on being long gone from our wild camp location by then. The first job of the day was to make a hasty phone call home to see whether Wayne's parents would drive out and meet us somewhere along the day's route to bring us our 3-season down sleeping bags, which we desperately needed. I was in two minds about ringing them, as I did not want to put them to any inconvenience, but Wayne pointed out that the further north we go, towards the Cheviots, the colder it would get. Better to bring them now on Day 2, which is closer to home, than have to drive to the Scottish borders in a couple of weeks. True, and Wayne's parents were fine about helping us out.

Figure 15 – Support Team and Heading to Bleaklow

By the time we had met up with our newly designated 'Support Team' at Snake Pass and refuelled on their picnic supplies, it was after midday before we set off again. We headed through Devil's Dike to Bleaklow Head, which was quite hard going on the feet because of stony trails. The fortunate thing about walking through moorland though is that there aren't any stinging nettles. The downside on the other hand are swarms of midges forever on the attack!

After what seemed like a long day getting used to the weight of our packs, we made it to our campsite at Crowden by 5:00 PM. The Caravan & Camping Club campsite is really well maintained with lovely flat pitches and spotless kitchen and bathroom facilities. What makes it even better is that the walk-up price is cheaper than what is quoted online. There is even a well-stocked camp shop, where we bought a couple of free-range eggs to go with our dinner. Refreshed after showering and looking forward to a good night's sleep in our warmer bags, thanks to our Support Team, we were now much better equipped to continue with our Pennine Way adventure.

Day 3 – Crowden to Standedge (12.5 miles) – 'In Fair Weather, Prepare for Foul'

We set off on day 3 fully refreshed and raring to go, especially after a hot bowl of porridge and a cuppa. We set off across the moors from Crowden, stopping at Black Hill for lunch. It was a tougher day with a lot of elevation change, but the trails were good, and we found we had a steadier pace and were getting more accustomed to our packs. Maybe because we had eaten some more of the food rations and off-loaded a tiny bit of the weight!

Figure 16 – Leaving Crowden and Black Hill Trig Point

The weather was fine for England. (We did not actually realise how lucky we were, as the following day's 17 miles were a wet and windy trudge in complete white-out.) Heading down Dean Clough and continuing on the section past Wessenden Reservoir, we were still smiling, despite the presence of midges once again. We reached our next campsite behind the Carriage House Pub at 5:00 PM exactly. We still had no blisters after hiking 28.5 miles in three days. So far, so good! It was another camp dinner of instant noodles and pork sausage, then an early night for both us.

Day 4 – Standedge to Jack's Bridge (17.7 miles) – 'A Slab of Spam'

Today was our first experience of rain. Not just a shower, but a constant downpour that both tests your waterproof gear to its limits and puts a dampener on your spirits. I guess it was the kind of rain that England is famous for. Taking your tent down in the rain and packing things away wet

Personal Experience 135

is no fun. It is even less fun getting your trail shoes soaked first thing in the morning, which leads to your feet squelching all day long. However, we had to accept that we would get rain some time or other during our hike along the Pennines.

Our first major landmark was White Hill, which was a complete white-out due to the miserable weather. We soldiered on regardless and were buoyed by the sight of a burger van, as we came to cross the A672, and warmed ourselves up with a good strong mug of Yorkshire tea. The owner, a rather generous Yorkshireman, assured us he was famous in these parts, his burger van pitch having been cited in a number of Pennine Way guidebooks. Well, he certainly made the day brighter for us by giving us some free sausage rolls and a slab of Spam to fry up for breakfast.

Figure 17 – Burger Van and Stoodley Pike

Grateful for our freebies – never ones to turn down food, not even spam – we headed on past Windy Hill and crossed the bridge that takes you over the M62. The weather still had not improved when we reached Blackstone Edge. It was that bleak you could not see further than 100 feet ahead. The one good thing about the trail was that we had nice stone slabs to walk on instead of trudging through bog. Around midday, we nipped in the White Horse Pub for a swift half, a pub literally in the middle of nowhere but perfectly placed so that we could dry off and warm up a bit. After passing some reservoirs, we reached Stoodley Pike, a giant stone tower high on a hillside, a beacon that can be seen for miles around.

The final stretch of the day was a drier walk to our campsite at Jack's Bridge, just outside the little touristy town of Hebden Bridge. This uphill stretch offered the traditional Pennine Way route or Wainwright's alternative. We opted to go the traditional way, which was a bad choice having had a tough uphill slog of 16 miles already. After braving several overgrown tracks covered with nettles, we finally arrived at the campsite at 6.30 PM. We were glad to get our wet gear off and change into something dry. Too tired to even walk to the nearby farm shop for supplies, Wayne fried up our slab of spam, which we enjoyed in a wrap with brown sauce, before snuggling down in our sleeping bags for a much needed sleep.

Day 5 – Rest Day at Hebden Bridge – 'Time for a Full English'

Day 5 was a rest day of sorts. One, because we had planned on having a lie-in after so many 6:00 AM alarm calls and, two, because our campsite was named 'Hebden Bridge Camping', we thought we would be close to town with minimal walking. In fact, it was a 4-mile round trip as the campsite is situated in a village outside the town, named Jack's Bridge.

Figure 18 – Hebden Bridge and Butcher Shop

We walked into town to find a launderette for some much needed clothes washing. We also had the task of acquiring a new sleeping mat for Wayne as his had burst beyond repair on the third night of this trip. Having slept on the floor on a pile of clothes for the last two nights, he assured me it was neither the most comfortable nor the warmest of things. Along with these mundane tasks, we were well and truly in need of two extra special FEBs ('Full English Breakfasts'). We devoured these in Frankie's Cafe, where we also made good use of the free Wi-Fi to update our blog.

After all the necessities were taken care of, there was still time for us to have a wander around to see the sights. Hebden is a lovely town filled with an array of touristy trinket shops and upmarket cafes. In the centre, opposite a quaint traditional English tea shop, there is a fantastic butcher's where we picked up some gourmet sausages. We had no idea when we arrived, but the town was also gearing up for the Tour de France competitors cycling through on the first weekend of July, so there was lots of cycling regalia everywhere.

Day 6 – Jack's Bridge to Ponden (10.2 miles) – 'Midge Attack'

After leaving camp at a respectable 10:30 AM, we deviated off the Pennine Way track just a little in order to visit the village farm shop we had heard so much about – the aptly named 'May's Aladdin's Cave'. And it really was! The tiny shop is stocked to the brim with everything you could possibly wish for as a hiker. We did not stick to our plan of only buying essentials but splurged on citronella candles to try and combat the midges (unfortunately, we found out later that they do not work) and two slabs of chocolate flapjack for our first rest break. Finally, we got going and soon found our pace again after yesterday's break.

Figure 19 – May's Aladdin's Cave and Heading for Wadsworth Moor

Personal Experience

We set off over Heptonstall Moor as the weather picked up a little. Well, actually a lot, compared to Friday's wash out. We reached Wadsworth Moor, then continued on passing the Walshaw Dean Reservoirs. The highlight of our day was reaching Top Withens, where a farmhouse stands in ruins. Said to have been the inspiration for the Brontë sisters when writing their popular novel 'Wuthering Heights', this is an extremely popular spot with day hikers and Japanese tourists in particular. We stopped for lunch and waited for a large tour group to depart, so we could photograph it, minus people.

Figure 20 – Top Withens and Trail Sign

Then, we continued on through dry, brown moorland to Ponden, where we camped in an overgrown field at the back of a guesthouse. It was rustic, to say the least, but we could not complain as we had it all to ourselves. We managed to finally dry out the tent and air our sleeping bags before the midges appeared in stealth mode. With our citronella candles failing miserably, Wayne hastily cooked up some instant noodles, before we hid in the tent and called it a night.

Day 7 – Ponden to Thornton-in-Craven (14.1 miles) – 'At Home in The Country'

The first thing we can confirm is that hiking the Pennine Way makes you constantly hungry. We have never denied that we both have big appetites, and food plays a large part in why we travel. We love to sample local delicacies everywhere we visit. Technically, it's good to be hungry, as hiking 16 miles uses approximately 1,750 calories. For this mammoth 268-mile walk, we should be consuming at least 4,000 calories per day, but even with all of our lightweight, simple cook, processed food, we are struggling to consume even 3,000 calories a day.

Today's walk was one of our favourites so far on the route. It was a hike through a number of different villages, giving me the perfect opportunity to nosey at some houses – one of my favourite pastimes. We enjoyed the beautiful morning sun rising over Ponden Reservoir. Then, the first section of the walk took us through farmers' fields to a village named Cowling, which entailed a lot of up and down over stiles and going through gates. It was fantastic weather for walking and the English countryside was at its best. Cowling seemed a lovely village and we understood instantly why the mantra on their town sign simply says "You'll Never Leave".

Figure 21 – Country House and Best Weather for Walking

Ever better, a little further on was the village of Lothersdale. We were completely wowed by its idyllic location and beautiful views of the countryside and both agreed that if we win the lottery, this would be an ideal place to live. The next section of the walk was mainly uphill to Pinhaw at 388 metres. It is the highest point around, so it offered us a great 360° view of the Yorkshire Dales from up there.

140   *Personal Experience*

Figure 22 – Looking down onto Lothersdale and Pennine Way Signage

By 5:00 PM, we had made it to Thornton-in-Craven, another picturesque village, but sadly lacking in a shop and a pub (so we definitely couldn't consider living there). We camped at Thornton Hall Farm Country Park, with a nice, freshly mowed campsite. It was just a shame there weren't any showers. We could not really complain as there is no other campsite off the Pennine Way for miles around, and we did have the camp field all to ourselves. It was a lovely, sunny evening, so we sat out on the grass to enjoy the sunset.

Day 8 – Thornton-in-Craven to Malham (15.1 miles) – 'Gargrave Grabs Top Spot'

Today, the weather was glorious. Wearing shorts and a T-shirt for the first time, it was a peaceful start hiking along the Leeds and Liverpool Canal, where we took our time to admire the collection of narrow boats moored at East Marton. We reached the quaint village of Gargrave (our new favourite) by 11:00 AM and popped into the Dalesman Cafe for a 'beaker of tea' served in cute Pennine Way hiker cups. The cafe also doubles up as a vintage sweetshop with Georgina's Gardinaria around the back. The cafe is popular with Pennine Way hikers, as it has an important landmark outside – a sign indicating that we have hiked 70 miles already from Edale, with 186 miles to go to reach Kirk Yetholm. (Not quite accurate with our own GPS route tracking, but there is always disparity with mileage depending on which route and optional side trips you decide to take.)

Figure 23 – Leeds & Liverpool Canal and Dalesman Cafe

From the cafe, we moved on to the local Co-op store to resupply with food for the next couple of days, putting our packs in a trolley and pushing them around to the bemusement of staff and customers. The rest of the walk basically took us through beautiful meadows following the River Aire. This kind of walking also came with a lot of nettles, which is not a good combination when wearing shorts. We had a rest stop at Airton, then continued on to the village of Malham. Malham is popular with day trippers due to the impressive limestone cliffs at Malham Cove.

We were shattered by the last couple of miles. My feet were killing me as I had acquired a blister from hell on my fourth toe after our 'soggy feet' episode, which was getting worse despite our supply of good blister plasters. We reached Townhead Farm Campsite around 5:00 PM, just before hordes of students on an outdoor expedition descended on the camp. We obviously chose the most popular campsite in the village. There was a big queue at the showers, but all was good in the world again when we sat down to a feast of sausage and black pudding cobs for tea. Did I mention that today we also went through 46 gates and climbed over 19 stiles? Yes, we did actually count them as we went along.

Day 9 – Malham to Horton-in-Ribblesdale (17.3 miles) – 'Up Down, Up Down'

Our big accomplishment today was reaching the end of the Pennine Way southern section. (That's one Harvey map ready to post home.) According to our GPS tracker, which includes to and from campsites, we have walked 102.9 miles already. We were really looking forward to this day as the itinerary included going up Pen-y-Ghent, one of the famous Yorkshire three peaks. We left the campsite at Malham after our usual breakfast and headed straight up to the top of the limestone cliffs known as Malham Cove. It was just as the guidebook had described, there were fantastic views from the top looking straight down the valley.

Figure 24 – Setting off for Malham Cove and View from the Top

Next, we hiked over to Malham Tarn, a high mountain lake, but this was quickly superseded by Fountains Fell, at 668 metres, the highest point so far, which we reached before lunch. The whole day was a series of reaching a high point, going down the other side, then across the valley to the next mountain to do it all over again. I topped up on painkillers for my blister, and we psyched ourselves up for heading up Pen-y-Ghent. We had two steep sections to tackle ascending up the southern ridge, which required a bit of scrambling to reach the top. The actual climb was not as bad as it looks from afar, and the fact that both steep sections have stone slabs going up really helps. At 694m, we could see the other two Yorkshire peaks, Ingleborough and Whernside. After speaking to others we passed hiking

Personal Experience 143

the Pennine Way, it sounds like we were lucky that the rain held off, and that we had any view at all, although we did experience extremely high winds at the top.

Figure 25 – Cairn on Fountains Fell and Pen-y-Ghent Cafe

Leaving Pen-y-Ghent, it was a long, long gravel track down the other side to reach Horton-in-Ribblesdale. We expected the day's mileage to be around 14 miles, but in fact we did over 17. Some miscalculation somewhere – as seems to be the norm on the Pennine Way. What brightened up the walk was when Wayne rescued a sheep that had got its head and horns stuck through a fence. As there was no farmer around, we just could not leave it in distress. It was our good deed to end the day. When we reached Horton-in-Ribblesdale, we popped into the Pen-y-Ghent Cafe for a cup of tea and an ice-cream before pitching our tent just down the road at the olde-worlde Holme Farm Campsite.

Day 10 – Horton-in-Ribblesdale to Hawes (17 miles) – 'The Never Ending Cam Road'

We left camp at 8.30 AM and set off for Hawes. We were in high spirits, knowing a rest day was ahead of us as well as a chippy! (The lady in the Pen-y-Ghent Cafe had informed us of its existence.) It was a walk along a hard, stony road that seemed to go on for miles, which was really hard going on the feet. Oh how we wished to be back on the moors again. The Cam High Road never seemed to end. We were both in pain, me hobbling along with my blisters and Wayne with an ache in his lower leg. We kept plodding on, having only two quick rest stops, eager to reach Hawes and get set up at the campsite.

We reached Hawes late afternoon, and it was perfect timing for us. Tour de France fever had hit the Dales. We had planned a rest day there anyhow, but it just so happened to coincide with the Tour de France weekend. So not only did we get to sample some fine cheese at the Wensleydale Creamery, but we, too, got swept up with the excitement in the village and stayed an extra day to see the competitors cycle through. There was bunting and bicycles everywhere. Shop fronts were decorated with cycling regalia, and local houses were trimmed up. We decided right away to stay for two rest days and make the most of visiting Hawes on this special weekend. Our only possible problem was securing a tent pitch on such a busy weekend. Luckily, the campsite we picked, Bainbridge Ings, never turns away hikers, and they were more than happy to extend our stay.

Figure 26 – Arrival at Hawes Village and Tour de France Fever

After a lovely hot shower, we headed straight to the centre of town to find the long awaited chip shop. We could tell it was really popular, as the adjoining cafe was full, and the takeaway had a queue winding out of the door and down the street. We waited patiently unable to decide what to have. In the end, we settled on large chips and battered black pudding. Great northern grub! We also splashed out on a bottle of wine, which we enjoyed back at the tent before nodding off, even though it was still light

Personal Experience

outside. One thing that can be said about hiking is it certainly helps you sleep!

Day 11 – Rest Day at Hawes (1) – 'Never Too Much Cheese Indulgence'

Today was definitely a day of indulgence. For once, we could get fresh supplies, so out went the camping rations as we headed off to the butcher's for some local produce. It was fried eggs for breakfast instead of the usual porridge, pork pie for lunch, and gourmet burgers for dinner. Not forgetting the couple of slabs of Wensleydale cheese we picked up from the Creamery. Now, this is the kind of camping that I love!

Figure 27 – Wensleydale Cheese Factory and Cheese Samples

Hawes is famous for having the Wensleydale Cheese Factory located right in the village. We could not resist going along to try some samples and thought it would be interesting to see how the cheese is made as there is a viewing gallery into the production area. We visited the Creamery in the morning, as this is the best time to see the production process in action. Our favourite part of the experience was the 'cheese tasting room'. Around 20 different varieties of cheese are available for you to try before you buy. We could not help but visit the tasting room twice! In our opinion, you can never over-indulge in cheese, especially Wensleydale.

Day 12 – Rest Day at Hawes (2) – 'Swept Up with Tour de France Fever'

It was not an early start for us, unlike the rest of the campsite guests that headed up the 'Buttertubs' road from 6:00 AM onwards for a good viewing spot to see who would be 'King of the Hill'. Instead, we enjoyed our first lie-in in ages and bought some more free-range eggs, so we could treat ourselves to omelettes for breakfast.

Figure 28 – Villagers Waiting Eagerly and Peloton Pedaling Past

The cyclists were not scheduled to reach Hawes village until just after 2:00 PM, so we had plenty of time to find a good place to watch. Just before they were due to cycle through, we headed to the edge of the village along the roadside, which was a great spot recommended by the campsite. The crowds cheered and clapped. The cyclists pedalled as fast as they could. And that was that! They flew past in a matter of seconds. Blink and you would have missed it. It was a great atmosphere though and a welcome break from the Pennine Way for a couple of days to rest our feet.

Day 13 – Hawes to Keld (13.2 miles) – 'Soaking Up the Dales'

It was time to get back on the trail after two much needed rest days. With our aches and pains almost gone, our feet revived, food rations stocked up, and our spirits lifted, we were set for continuing up north. The highlight of the next three days for us would be reaching the halfway point on the Pennine Way. This is officially marked by the Tan Hill Inn, the highest pub in Great Britain, providing us with a perfect photo opportunity and chance for a pint along the way.

We won't lie, getting up early and getting back on the trail was hard. The bags somehow seemed heavier whilst our feet seemed slower, and we still had such a long way to go. It did not help matters that to start the day, we knew we would be walking uphill for the first 6 miles. It was an uphill walk that was opposite the Buttertubs Hill, the one that the cyclists had powered up yesterday to see who was 'King of the Hill' – one word – a 'killer' of a hill! We powered on and made it to the top of Great Shunner Fell. At 716 metres, it was the highest point we had reached so far and a good place to stop for lunch. It was a rare treat to have Wensleydale cheese with cranberries in today's wraps, which were delicious.

We set off again, reaching our next stop along the way, the village of Thwaite. We were glad of a coffee shop joined to the hotel as our feet were aching from walking 2 miles along a stone track. The next section from Thwaite to Keld was one of the most scenic of the journey so far, especially as we had good weather. Blue skies and fluffy clouds always make for a good photo. Wayne even took the opportunity to stop on the hillside to capture a time lapse sequence of the moving clouds and the intermittent sun. It was a perfect spot looking down the valley onto the village of Muker, where a festival was in full swing.

Figure 29 – Hills & Pastures and Hillside Photography

Personal Experience

We continued on to Keld along the high route, which, although scenic, presented us with lots of obstacles. Dodging ferns and boulders made a 13-mile day seem unusually long, which was not what we really wanted on a day that was already hard going on the feet with lots of ascent. We arrived in Keld well after 6:00 PM and stayed at Rukins Park Lodge Campsite. They have a great deal for walkers, as it is only £5 per person, including hot showers. There is also a cafe and small shop, which is where you should book your pitch, but this was closing by the time we arrived. We were that tired, we did not even walk up the hill to the main field to pitch our tent. Instead, we opted for a patch of grass near the entrance gate. We soon got the tent up, so we could escape the midges.

Day 14 – Keld to Clove Lodge, Baldersdale (14.5 miles) – 'Entering Bog Zone at The Halfway Point'

From Keld, in beautiful Swaledale, we said goodbye to the Yorkshire Dales and made it to the Tan Hill Inn by 11:30 AM, which was already bustling with walkers. We found out that it is not just the highest pub in England, but, in fact, the highest pub in Great Britain. (There is a Guinness World Record Certificate to prove it!) It also is the official halfway point on the Pennine Way. As it was early, we opted for a mug of tea instead of a pint to celebrate this milestone and made use of the Wi-Fi. Yes, even in the middle of nowhere it is possible to get on the internet – sometimes.

Figure 30 – Heading to the Tan Hill Inn and Crossing Bog on Stepping Stones

Personal Experience

Looking across to the Tan Hill Inn, we should not have been surprised that it really is the only sign of civilisation for miles around. We set off again around midday and found ourselves entering Durham, an unknown territory for us. Unfortunately, we also found ourselves entering 'bog zone' for the first time. Durham Council had not seen fit to provide us with a lovely slabbed pathway (as is the case in the preceding areas on the Pennine Way), so that we could cross the moors without getting our feet wet. As a result, we had to make our own way across the dreaded bog as best as we could.

After crossing a dodgy section of very boggy ground, we were thankful that the next part was mostly walking across farmland and meadows, before we reached the A66 underpass. We then continued on to Clove Lodge, our destination for the night, which is a farm guesthouse with camping barn right next to the Pennine Way at Baldersdale. (Although it had an ominous 'For Sale' sign up at the time of our walking, making us question its future existence.) We just wanted a spot to pitch our tent, so they offered us private use of a little enclosed garden area, plus the facilities of a vacant guest room ensuite, for £5 each. It was perfect for us, apart from the ever-present midges. The only other downside of being campers was a very wet tent in the morning, as it had rained all through the night.

Day 15 – Clove Lodge to Middleton-in-Teesdale to Wild Camp (13.1 miles) – 'Just a Bit Further'

We set the alarm for 6:00 AM, hoping to be away early. But, as we wanted the tent to dry off before we left and to avoid the midges at first light, we ended up having a lazy morning and did not set off until 10:00 AM.

After climbing over lots of stiles and going through lots of gates (again), our first port of call was Middleton-in-Teesdale. We spent a couple of hours in town to resupply with food. Then, we were going to push on and find a suitable wild camp spot for the night, so we would have less miles to walk the following day. When we left Middleton, we were surprised to see a sign indicating that we were only 23 miles from Scotch Corner. Wow, as a major junction of the A1 and A66 trunk roads and an extremely well known place in the UK, that really helped put into perspective how far we had already walked. Following the River Tees, we had a spring in our step as we continued on, despite the bags being heavier once again now that we had restocked with all sorts of goodies.

Figure 31 – Swing Bridge over River Tees and PW Information Board

We managed to find what we thought was a good wild camp spot just after the quarry beyond the Low and High Force waterfalls. I say *thought* because after the wind had dropped and the sun went down, it was attack of the midges yet again. Luckily, the rain that had been forecast held off and our spirits remained high.

Day 16 – Wild Camp to Dufton (14.7 miles) – 'Good Old Nick'

It was a swift get up and go as we set the alarm for a 5:00 AM start so that we could try to sneak off before another major attack of the midges. Wondering why they seem to love us so much, we later found out from the internet that they are attracted to our carbon dioxide, as well as dark colours and sheltered environments. No wonder they love hovering around our tent, backpacks, and *us* so much. Breathing out carbon dioxide all night in a closed environment, such as a tent, is just the invitation midges need to have a good old party. Of course, when we pitched our tent at the wild camp spot, the first thing we looked for was a sheltered area out of the wind. Bad move! Now that we know the facts, we will be much more midge aware.

Personal Experience

Our early morning walk followed the River Tees once more, which proved not to be the gentle stroll along the river that we were expecting. There was some manageable scrambling over boulders as we came upon the impressive waterfall and giant dam that appeared at Cauldron Snout. The highlight of the day was undoubtedly High Cup Nick, a classic U-shaped glacial valley that simply took our breath away. As it was a bright, sunny day, the views down the valley were simply stunning. The actual U-shape of the valley is so large that it is hard to fit it in its entirety on your camera screen, unless you have a wide angle lens. It was our favourite spot on the Pennine Way so far!

Figure 32 – Cauldron Snout and High Cup Nick

We had a 'selfie' shot in front of the valley and picked a spot for lunch where we could enjoy the view, along with lots of other day walkers, the most we have seen along the route so far. As we left High Cup Nick, we saw wild horses while making our way down off the mountain. However, the best sight of all was the spectacular view off into the distance. It was such a clear day that we were able to see as far as the Yorkshire Dales to the left, as well as some of the famous peaks of the Lake District to the right.

Then, it was just a simple stroll downhill all the way into Dufton. It was an early arrival for us at the campsite. We reached the Grandie Caravan Park around 4:00 PM and promptly made use of the shower facilities in view of our wild camp the previous night. Arriving early also gave us chance to do some laundry and to buy some fresh eggs from the local cafe. There was even time for some last minute sunbathing and catching up with writing our blog diary. It was definitely a day on the Pennine Way to remember.

Day 17 – Dufton to Greg's Hut (9.4 miles) – 'The High Point'

Today was to be one of our shortest walking days. From Dufton to our destination, Greg's Hut (which is a bothy in the hills maintained by volunteers), it was only nine or so miles. This gave us the chance to have a more leisurely morning at the campsite instead of our usual get up, pack up, and go. We enjoyed a hearty breakfast and finally set off around 10.30 AM. Walking around Brownber Hill, it was a long, gradual uphill walk out of Dufton, which was fine apart from the section along a narrow track that was covered in nettles and swarming with midges, our favourite friends. As we continued up through farmland, we were able to watch some farmers rounding up the sheep with their trusty dogs, which was a welcome breather at that point.

Figure 33 – Trig Point atop Cross Fell and Greg's Hut Main Room

We headed up to Knock Old Man at 794 metres, then on to Great Dun Fell, unmissable for miles around due to the radar station with its numerous satellite dishes positioned on top. Then, we carried on further to Little Dun Fell at 842 metres, where we finally stopped for a break. The highest point of the day, however, was reaching the top of Cross Fell, which, at 893 metres, is the highest point on the entire Pennine Way. It was incredibly blustery up there, but a new shelter proved invaluable in shielding us from

Personal Experience

the penetrating wind. It was only a short distance from this point until we reached Greg's Hut, named in honour of John Gregory, a keen climber, who was killed by an avalanche in the Alps in 1968. His parents funded much of the restoration work of the hut in memory of their son, in conjunction with the Mountain Bothies Association.

As we had good weather, we chose not to stay inside the hut but rather preferred to pitch our tent in the garden out front. Although basic, we can see how the hut is invaluable for hikers when the weather turns, serving as a much needed place of shelter and respite. It can be very bleak out on the fells, with no sign of civilisation for miles around. After sheltering from the wind and cooking inside the bothy, we were treated to a great sunset to end the day. The other good thing about the hut is that there is no fee. So, much like a wild camp, we enjoyed a 'freebie' night but slept far more soundly without fear of being caught camping on private land.

Day 18 – Greg's Hut to Alston (10.5 miles) – 'Birthday B&B Pick Me Up'

We were in high spirits today as our destination, Alston, had been earmarked as a rest day the following day, because it was Wayne's birthday. It was quite an easy walk. The track was clearly marked and mostly flat. We reached the village of Garrygill, which was our halfway marker, in what seemed like no time, so we sat on the village green for a drink and a snack. We were looking forward to arriving in Alston by lunchtime, so we powered on, getting there around 1:00 PM. After doing a quick recce of the town (it was a lot smaller than what we were expecting), we headed to a nice, cosy cafe, where we treated ourselves to a proper lunch.

Alston was proving a winner until we headed to the only campsite in town, which did not fill us with much enthusiasm. Set at the back of a scrapyard, complete with some old sofas and a couple of rubbish skips outside the reception area, the place looked rather dodgy. As no one was around to check us in, we made a rash decision to get the hell out of there and book into a cheap and cheerful B&B we had spotted in town. It was Wayne's birthday the next day after all, so it did not take much convincing to decide to treat ourselves to a proper bed for one night after 17 nights of camping.

Figure 34 – Approaching Alston, cosy 'Cumbrian Pantry' Cafe, and Mini Pub Crawl

For £50 including full English breakfast, we checked in at the Victoria Inn, a B&B that doubles up as a pub and Indian restaurant. Birthday celebrations are not complete without a few beers, so as we were staying the night, we decided to have a mini pub crawl and celebrate Wayne's birthday a night early. We got changed and headed straight to the Turks Head, which felt like a 'locals' kind of pub, then moved on to the Angel Inn, which looked to be serving some fantastic bar meals, then finally settled in The Cumberland, which was recommended to us for serving 'real ales'. For such a small town, there was a large number of public houses to choose from.

As with all good things, there comes a price, and ours was forfeiting our planned rest day the following day. As we had spent extra on the B&B and because Alston did not really have enough to keep us occupied for an extra day without spending money, we decided to move on. We still had our miles to cover after all!

Day 19 – Alston to Greenhead (18 miles) – 'Think Positive, It Could Be Worse!'

The 12th July – Wayne's birthday! Usually, we'd be booked into some swanky restaurant for a 3-course meal, giving me the chance to wear a posh frock and hoping to dine al fresco. Instead, we were waking up in a

B&B, mentally preparing ourselves for the 18-mile walk ahead. Cue birthday blues, not just for Wayne, but for both of us! On the positive side, the slight hangover from pre-birthday drinks the night before was eased by the fantastic full English breakfast we were treated to downstairs in the pub. With our bodies refuelled and our backpacks re-loaded, we finally set off at 10:00 AM. Our destination for today: Greenhead.

Figure 35 – South Tynedale Railway and Yew Tree Chapel

We won't lie, it was a boring day! Neither of us was in the mood to walk 18 miles. We were constantly clockwatching and checking our mileage at every opportunity. The high point of the day was stopping at Slaggyford, where we sat on a park bench and had lunch. There was a lovely chapel with stained glass windows and a country garden that caught our eye. After that, we were literally walking through field after field after field. We just kept putting one foot in front of the other and ploughing on hoping to get there anytime soon.

We finally arrived at Holmhead Guesthouse & Camping Barn around 7:00 PM, just as it started to rain. It was a hurried pitch of the tent so we could take refuge out of the rain and away from the midges. The campsite is straight off the Pennine Way next to Thirlwall Castle. (The clue is in the name; there's literally a few walls left standing.) That night, we did not venture further than the little toilet/shower. Our motto for the day was 'it could be worse'. Indeed, it could have been raining all day and the campsite could have been full. At least, we had somewhere to wash, rest, and sleep. PMA – positive mental attitude!

Day 20 – Greenhead to Hadrian's Wall to Forest Wild Camp (11 miles) – 'Less Than 100 Miles to Go!'

Because of heavy rain through the night, we did not set off as early as we had planned, as we waited for the tent to dry out. After finally leaving the campsite nearer to midday, we were straight back on the Pennine Way heading for Hadrian's Wall, a defensive fortification from Roman Britain and now a UNESCO World Heritage Site. The day became a bit of a geography and history lesson rolled into one.

Figure 36 – Hadrian's Wall

Stretching across the north of England for 84 miles, Hadrian's Wall, or rather the ruins that remain, runs from Bowness-on-Solway in Cumbria on the west coast to Wallsend on Tyneside on the east coast. As part of the Pennine Way, we got to walk alongside several miles of it, taking in some breathtaking scenery, as the wall passes through rugged moorland. We also got to meet and chat with a lot of long-distance hikers walking in the opposite direction. With less than 100 miles to go, we had a lot to talk about.

We expected a 'flat' straightforward walk – Romans built straight roads after all – but Hadrian's Wall follows the contours of the hills, so you find yourself walking a constant up and down. There are some particularly sharp ascents and descents after passing Milecastle 41, so it was not an easy walk after all. We wanted to go further than the campsite at Once Brewed, otherwise it would have been a really short day. So we pushed on looking for a place where we could wild camp for the night. Eventually, we found a great spot after Stonefolds, where you enter the forest. It was down an old stone track that had been fenced off and left to grow wild.

Day 21 – Wild Camp to Bellingham (11.3 miles) – 'An Unexpected Kindness'

In the morning, we hiked around 3 miles through forest and farmland, which meant we got wet feet because of the morning dew, before we stopped for breakfast and got the tent out to dry. Later in the day, we had an unexpected rest stop at Horneystead Farm, which is right on the Pennine Way route. There was a sign on the gate welcoming walkers to the shed in the farmyard, which on entering we discovered was filled with all sorts of goodies.

Figure 37 – Walkers Welcome and Horneystead Farm Shed

Tea, coffee, chocolate bars, crisps, soup, and a fridge full of cold drinks. You could help yourself to anything and leave a donation in an honesty tin. Wow! What an unexpected kindness and welcome relief on a hot day! There was a table and chairs, an old sofa to sit on and rest our feet, as well as a heater to warm you up on a cold day. It was completely awesome! There was no one around to thank personally, so we left a message on the notepad provided, saying a huge thank you to Horneystead Farm as their goodie shed really made our day!

Feeling revived and full of appreciation, we continued on to Bellingham. We passed the Caravan & Camping Club site on the outskirts of Bellingham, continuing along the main road, then took a shortcut along the river to town, where we finally reached our home for the night at Demesne Farm Campsite. We found ourselves a nice flat pitch and set to work on washing all of our clothing by hand. We were desperate for clean clothes, and it had been a while since we had found a launderette or had a campsite with laundry facilities.

We also had to go into town and resupply with food and gas for our final 3 days on the Pennine Way. Yes, Bellingham really is the last place to stock up. By the time we got back, it was raining, so we grabbed all the washing off the line and took refuge in the 'drying room'. What a great place to hang out! We got the log burning stove going, which not only dried our clothes but kept us warm whilst we also charged our electronics, making use of the power socket in there.

Day 22 – Bellingham to Byrness (15.7 miles) – 'Are We There Yet?'

It wasn't a quick get away from Bellingham as we spent a while chatting to a fellow camper. We learned that the guy had spent a few years travelling around South America, so there began a mammoth swapping of travel tales. It's amazing who you meet and the stories you hear along the trail.

Finally on our way, we made a big mistake by opting to take an 'Alternative Pennine Way Path'. It was at a junction after crossing farmland. The traditional route seemed to veer uphill, so we took the alternative as it appeared the better, flatter path. Unfortunately, it led us straight into bog, resulting in wet feet for the remainder of the day. After getting clear of the bog, the sun had disappeared and the sky was looking very overcast. With our morale running low, we were pleasantly surprised by the poster offering free camping in the garden at the Forest View Inn. The only catch, you had to purchase a two-course meal for £10.

Well, hot home-cooked food versus something from a packet with added water. Hmm, it was a no brainer! I dialled the phone number and booked right away. You have never seen two people's moods change as rapidly as ours. With the thought of a great meal ahead, we continued on with a very noticeable spring in our step. On the way to Byrness, we passed Border Forest Park Campsite, which is the place we would have stayed at if we had not seen the poster advertising the Forest View Inn.

Figure 38 – Forest View Inn and Cheers!

When we finally reached Byrness, we turned left at the church and walked along a footpath to the inn, which is situated in the main part of the village. It's effectively three houses joined together, providing rooms for B&B guests, with a huge conservatory on the back where walkers can mingle. The enclosed rear garden doubles up for camping, with a separate washroom and drying room facilities for campers, too. We couldn't have hoped for anything better. The hospitality of the owners, Colin and Joyce, was also first-rate. Having arrived looking slightly weary, we were immediately welcomed and offered a hot drink and comfy seat.

There's a great atmosphere about the place with hikers from all backgrounds, ages, and continents mixing and sharing stories and experiences. The highlight of the night was the home-cooked food. We were invited into the dining room around 7.30pm to our own candle lit table. It was lovely, but there was no time for etiquette as we proceeded to devour each course that was laid before us. We retired to the tent satisfied, knowing that we were almost at the end. Tomorrow, we would be stepping into Scotland, with only one more night to go.

Day 23 – Byrness to 2nd Mountain Hut (18 miles) – 'The Hardest Day'

Little did we know that today was to be our hardest day hiking the Pennine Way. Not only did we have to contend with rain, but there was also a lot of elevation change which we weren't expecting. As we set off from Byrness, we found ourselves facing a mammoth uphill trudge through a forest of ferns. Luckily, we managed to avoid the rain all morning and set a good pace over the flat sections of the walk, reaching the first mountain rescue hut by midday. We took respite in the bothy for an hour, eating our lunch and resting our feet in preparation for the next 9 miles. Lamb Hill was our halfway point for the day.

As we walked higher, the inevitable happened. The clouds came in, and it started to rain. So out of our backpacks came our full waterproofs, which we had now only put on for the third time since starting the trip back in June. Windy Gyle was true to its name, as it was blowing a gale down the valley, which nearly knocked us off our feet. Despite the rain, it was much drier across the Cheviots than what we expected. Having heard many horror stories about people getting stuck in bog up to their knees, we found the ground to be remarkably dry, with most of the trail now slabbed across the worst sections. We both wondered how boggy it would have been for the original Pennine Wayers way back in 1965.

Figure 39 – Border Fence between England & Scotland and 2nd Mountain Hut

As there was so much up and down which was hard on the knees, we decided not to make it even harder on ourselves by the addition of walking up the Cheviot peak. It's an extra mile and a quarter off the Pennine Way route, plus the same to return to the trail. With such bad weather preventing any views from the top, we weren't desperate to bag another peak. We'll save that one for another time. We continued on, heading for the second mountain hut, which is where we planned on staying overnight to break up the final section of the walk.

We arrived a little after 6:00 PM as the sun disappeared. Thinking we'd be the only guests for the night, we made ourselves at home and feasted on soup and instant noodles for dinner – our final food rations. Shattered from the day's events, we settled down ready to sleep around 8:30 PM when there was a sudden knock at the door. Another couple had reached the hut, seeking refuge after walking 28 miles that day. We moved around to make space for them, then woke at 4:30 AM to find them leaving already. Now that really is hardcore!

Day 24 – 2nd Mountain Hut to Kirk Yetholm (7.5 miles) – '268 Miles, Job Done!'

Today was the day we would finally cross into Scotland. We could see it yesterday, having walked alongside it for the best part of the day. But there was a fence creating a barrier the entire time. It seemed strange. The fence topped with barbed wire on some sections was either keeping the English out or not letting the Scots in. Whereas it was dull and miserable for us, it seemed much brighter on the Scottish side as the sun was trying to break through. Finally, there was a stile giving us access over the wall. We had entered Scotland at last!

We had approximately four and a half miles left to reach Kirk Yetholm. To make for an easier morning, we chose to take the alternative 'low' Pennine Way route into the village, which saved us at least half a mile and several ups and downs. Then, there it was, off in the distance, as we were about to embark on our final mile of this incredibly journey – Kirk Yetholm!

Figure 40 – Kirk Yetholm and Border Hotel

We reached Kirk Yetholm at 11:00 AM. Despite looking around carefully, we didn't find an official 'End of the Pennine Way' trail sign. The only sign we discovered signalling we had reached the finish was high on the wall of the Border Hotel. The bar didn't open until 11:30 AM, so we sat outside for half an hour and rested our feet until we could order some drinks. We had been told along the way that the Border Hotel no longer stands a free pint for Pennine Wayers at the finish, so we were surprised that we were presented with both a certificate and a free pint when we mentioned we had just completed it! We couldn't quite believe what we'd accomplished – actually walking to Scotland. The Pennine Way is truly an epic undertaking and a real test of your mettle. But what an incredible journey on foot and amazing adventure we'd had over the Pennine hills of England!

Figure 41 – End of Pennine Way and Finisher Surprise

Personal Experience   163

Appendices

A. Checklists

These checklists are meant to assist you with your preparations. Depending on the month you are hiking and your personal preferences, you can add or remove certain items from the lists. For those who are unsure about what to pack: if you stick to the lists, you will be in good shape.

Clothing ( ) indicates optional items

	Hiking socks		Rain jacket
	Underwear		Hat or visor
	Shorts		Beanie/warm hat
	Long trousers/pants (hiking or jogging)		Trail hiking shoes/boots
	Long sleeve T-shirt		Gloves
	Short sleeve T-shirt		Sleepwear
	Fleece jacket or synthetic insulated jacket (mid-layer)	( )	Long underwear
	Wind shirt/jacket	( )	Flip-flops/camp shoes

Personal Items (optional)

	Notepad, pen		Mirror
	Highlighter pen (if you want to draw route on your map)		Tripod
	E-reader, Book, Guidebook		Radio/ Music player, headphones

Gear ( ) indicates optional items

	Backpack		Money
	Tent/bivy/tarp	( )	Shovel
	Sleeping bag		Sunglasses
	Sleeping pad		Toilet paper
	Stove		Towel
	Fuel		Head lamp
	Spark striker/lighter		Watch
	Pot	( )	Trekking poles
	Long spoon/utensils	( )	Sleeping gear (ear plugs, inflatable pillow, etc.)
	Food & snacks	( )	Spare water container (collapsible)
	Water treatment	( )	Medication
	Hydration pack or bottles	( )	Deodorant
	Mug (with lid)	( )	Insect repellent
	Pocket knife	( )	Moisturiser
	First aid kit		Compass
	Silver survival blanket	( )	GPS watch
	Sunscreen (SPF 30 & up)	( )	Sewing kit
	Lip balm (with SPF)	( )	Fishing rod
	Tooth brush and paste		
	Soap (biodegradable)		
	Camera		
	Extra batteries & memory card(s)		
	Photo ID/passport		
	Printouts for all travel arrangements		
	Map or map app		

Appendices 165

Food List per Day per Person (3 alternatives per meal)

Breakfast
2 slices of bread and peanut butter
2 cups muesli/granola + ½ cup dried milk
2 eggs + 1 tortilla wrap

Lunch
Canned, dried, smoked meat + crackers
Fish in a pouch with 2 slices of bread
Hummus with 2 tortillas

Snacks
Nuts and seeds
Dried fruit
Protein/granola bars

Dinner
Freeze dried instant meal
1 packet of instant noodles, veggies + broth
1 pouch of tuna with packet of dried couscous

Other Food Items / Condiments

Sugar	
Coffee (and creamer)	
Tea	
Hot chocolate for evenings	
Olive oil	

Salt & pepper	
Spices & herbs, hot sauce, etc.	
Vitamins & minerals	
Parmesan cheese flakes	
Powdered milk	

B. Food Suggestions

Breakfast

- Instant oatmeal (purchase with or add flavours and sugar), porridge, semolina, and polenta with dried fruits
- Self-mixed cereals – with sesame, chia, flax, sunflower, pumpkin and other seeds; raisins and other dried fruit and berries; nuts; coconut flakes; rolled oats, shredded wheat, multi grains, etc.; mixed with dry milk, powdered soy, coconut, or almond milk, and possibly protein powder
- Pumpernickel (dark rye bread), tortilla, pita, or other dense, long-lasting breads
- Almond and peanut butter; tahini (sesame paste); chocolate spread; jam and honey
- Freeze dried breakfasts (e.g., scrambled egg, hash brown)
- Tea bags, tea pouches (such as ginger granulate), coffee, hot chocolate, sugar
- Fresh eggs (if you can carry them without breaking!)

Lunch

- Tinned meat, smoked/dried sausage (e.g., traditional salami), beef and other jerkies
- Tuna and salmon in pouches; tinned fish and mussels in sauces; dried salted fish and shrimp
- Hard boiled eggs
- Hummus; dried couscous (add boiling water)
- Crackers (wheat, whole grain, quinoa, corn); breads and tortillas
- Peanut butter; squeezy cheese; cheese triangles; pouches of olive oil and herbs; other veggie/vegan spreads
- Aged cheeses (repackaged in breathable material keep rather well)
- Pork pie; pasties; scotch eggs; ham (if you pass by a butchers and can buy fresh to eat that day)

Snacks

- Almonds, pistachios, other nuts and seeds (no shells, with/-out flavours, smoked)
- Dried fruits (mango, apricot, banana, date, fig, apple, etc.) and berries; fruit leather
- Power bars and gels; protein, granola, and cereal bars; other candy and snack bars
- Sundried tomatoes, veggie chips, olives in oil
- Dried corn kernels for popcorn in the evening (refine with oil, salt, sugar)
- Chocolate, jelly sweets, hard boiled sweets, fudge, (limit these 'empty calories')

Dinner

- Freeze dried instant meals in pouches – just add boiling water (try different varieties, flavours, and brands prior)
- Pasta with sundried tomatoes, tomato paste, and/or pesto, olive oil and spices, parmesan
- Quinoa, millet, and couscous with herbs and spices with packet tuna (add dried carrots, onion, peas)
- Soup base or stock cubes, add noodles or rice and flakes of mushroom, parsley, tomato, etc.
- Ramen noodles and other instant dishes (e.g., macaroni & cheese, dried mashed potatoes) with instant gravy
- Burritos with rice, packet chicken, beans, cheese, dried bell pepper
- Mixed lentils, beans, and chickpeas with seasoning (keep in mind the cooking times)
- Condiments: salt, pepper, spices, little sachets of mayonnaise, ketchup, hot sauce, soy sauce, olive oil, chilli flakes, parmesan
- Herbal tea, instant hot chocolate, hot lemon with honey

C. Campsite, Bunkhouse & Hostel Listing

Edale

Fieldhead Campsite, Edale, Hope Valley, Derbyshire, S33 7ZA
Tel: +44 1433 670386
Website: www.fieldhead-campsite.co.uk
Email: bookings@fieldhead-campsite.co.uk
Camping: £6.50 per person/night

Greenacres Camping and Caravan Site, Nether Booth, Edale, Derbyshire, S33 7ZH
Tel: +44 1433 670375 (9am-5pm, Monday-Saturday); +44 1433 670082 (Other times)
Website: www.greenacrescampsite.com
Email: enquiries@greenacrescampsite.com
Camping: £5 per person/night (Mmnimum £10 per night per tent)

Upper Booth Farm & Campsite, Edale, Hope Valley, Derbyshire, S33 7ZJ
Tel: +44 1433 670250
Website: www.upperboothcamping.co.uk
Email: mail@helliwell.info
Camping: £6 per person/night (£7 per person on Bank Holidays)
Camping barn: £8 per person/night (max. 12 people) or £90 for exclusive use of barn

Waterside Farm Camp Site, Barber Booth Road, Edale Hope Valley, Derbyshire, S33 7ZL
Tel: +44 1433 670215
Website: www.ukcampsite.co.uk
Email: jencooper@talk21.com
Camping: £5 per person/night

YHA Edale, Rowland Cote, Nether Booth, Edale, Hope Valley, Derbyshire, S33 7ZH
Tel: +44 845 371 9514
Email: edale@yha.org.uk
Website: www.yha.org.uk/hostel/edale
Beds in shared single sex rooms, adults: £19 - £30 depending on season; private room sleeps up to 2 people: £65 - £69

Hayfield

The Camping and Caravanning Club Site, Kinder Road, High Peak, Hayfield, Derbyshire, SK22 2LE
Tel: +44 1663 745394
Website: www.campingandcaravanningclub.co.uk/campsites/uk/derbyshire/highpeak/hayfield
Camping: From £6.30 to £10.65 per person/night

Torside

The Old House, Woodhead Road, Torside, Glossop, Derbyshire, SK13 1HU
Tel: +44 1457 857527
Website: www.oldhouse.torside.co.uk
Email: oldhouse@torside.co.uk

Bed & Breakfast, Double/Twin, en-suite, from £37.50 per person/per night
Pennine Way Package: Includes 2 nights stay, transport to and from walks or baggage transfers. Based on 2 people sharing a double or twin room, ensuite, £55 per person/night

Crowden

The Camping and Caravanning Club Site, Woodhead Road, Crowden, Glossop, Derbyshire, SK13 1HZ
Tel: +44 1457 866057
Website: www.campingandcaravanningclub.co.uk/campsites/uk/glossop/crowden
Camping: From £5.60 to £9.50 per person/per night

Standedge

The Carriage House, Manchester Road, Standedge, West Yorkshire, HD7 6NL
Tel: +44 1484 844419
Website: www.thecarriage-house.co.uk
Email:info@thecarriage-house.co.uk
Camping: £5.00 per person/night
Bed & Breakfast: £80 double room/ £50 single room, ensuite, includes breakfast

Mankinholes

YHA Mankinholes, Mankinholes, Todmorden, Lancashire, OL14 6HR
Tel: +44 1706 812340
Email: mankinholes@yha.org.uk
Website: www.yha.org.uk/hostel/mankinholes
Beds in shared single sex rooms, adults: £15; private room sleeps ups to 2 people: £29

Hebden Bridge

Badger Fields Farm, Badger Lane, Blackshaw Head, Hebden Bridge, W. Yorkshire, HX7 7JX
Tel: +44 1422 845161
Website: www.badgerfields.com
Email: badgerfields@hotmail.com
Camping: £5 per person/night
Bed & Breakfast: £34.00 per person/ night for two persons sharing. Single occupancy: £42.00 per night. Evening meals from: £15.00 per person for a two course meal. Packed lunches available at £6.50 each.

Hebden Bridge Hostel, The Birchcliffe Centre, Hebden Bridge, Yorkshire, HX7 8DG
Tel: +44 1422 843183
Website: www.hebdenbridgehostel.co.uk
Email: mama@hebdenbridgehostel.co.uk
Dorm bed £20/ Double room £60/ Twin room £55/ Bunk-Room bed: £14

New Delight Inn, Jack Bridge, Blackshaw Head, Hebden Bridge, West Yorkshire, HX7 7HT
Tel: +44 1422 844628
Website: www.newdelightinn.co.uk
Email:dan@newdelight.freeserve.co.uk
Camping: £5 per person/night

Colden

May's (Aladdin's Cave) Shop – Highgate Farm, Colden, Hebden Bridge, West Yorkshire, HX7 7PF
Tel: +44 1422 842897
Shop opening: 7am-9pm. Basic overnight camping (outside toilet & running water) is available next to the shop, free to Pennine Wayfarers.

Ponden/Stanbury

Ponden Guest House & Camping, Stanbury, Haworth, Keighley, W. Yorkshire, BD22 0HR
Tel: +44 1535 644154
Website: www.pondenhouse.co.uk
Email: brenda.taylor@pondenhouse.co.uk
Camping: £5.00 per person/per night (Breakfast: non-residents £7)
Bed & Breakfast: Double, en suite, £80, single occupancy £70, Twin single £50
Also available by arrangement: Evening meal £18 per person; packed lunch: £5.50

The Mill at Ponden, Ponden Mill, Scar Top Rd, Oldfield, Keighley, W. Yorkshire, BD22 0JR
Tel +44 1535 643923
Website: www.themillatponden.com
Email: richard@themillatponden.com
Camping: £10 per tent (2 People)

YHA Haworth, Longlands Drive, Lees Lane, Haworth, Keighley, West Yorkshire, BD22 8RT
Tel: +44 845 371 9520
Website: www.yha.org.uk/hostel/haworth
Email: haworth@yha.org.uk
Beds in shared single sex rooms, adults: £15 - £18 depending on season; private room sleeps ups to 2 people: £29 - £39

Cowling

Winter House Farm, Colne Road, Cowling, Keighley, West Yorkshire, BD22 0NN
Tel: +44 1535 632234
Website: www.ukcampsite.co.uk
Email: winterhouse1947@aol.com
Camping: £5.00 per person/night

Thornton-in-Craven

Thornton Hall Country Park, Thornton-in-Craven, nr Skipton, North Yorkshire BD23 3TS
Tel: +44 1282 841148
Website: www.thorntonhallcountrypark.co.uk
Camping: Tent (no electric) with 2 persons: £15

Earby

YHA Earby, 9-11 Birch Hall Lane, Earby, Barnoldswick, Lancashire, BB18 6JX
Tel: +44 845 371 9016
Website: www.yha.org.uk/hostel/earby

Email: earby@yha.org.uk
Beds in shared single sex rooms, adults: £15; private room sleeps ups to 2 people: £39

Gargrave

Eshton Road Caravan Park, Eshton road, Gargrave, Skipton, North Yorkshire, BD23 3PN
Tel: +44 1756 749229
Website: www.ukcampsite.co.uk
Camping: £5 per person/night

Malham

Hill Top Farm Bunkbarn, Malham, Skipton, North Yorkshire, BD23 4DJ
Tel: +44 1729 830320
Website: www.hilltopmalham.co.uk/bunkbarn-malham
Email: hello@hilltopmalham.co.uk
Individual beds: £20 per person/night (no letting of individual beds at weekends or during school holidays)

Riverside Campsite, Town Head Farm, Cove Road, Malham, Skipton, North Yorkshire, BD23 4DJ
Tel: +44 1729 830287
Website: www.malhamdale.com/camping.htm
NO email or web bookings available, telephone bookings only & no answerphone.
Camping: £7 per person/night

YHA Malham, Malham, Skipton, North Yorkshire, BD23 4DB
Tel: +44 845 371 9529
Website: www.yha.org.uk/hostel/malham
Email: malham@yha.org.uk
Beds in shared single sex rooms, adults: £15 - £30 depending on season; private room sleeps ups to 2 people: £39 - £49

Airton

Airton Friends' Meeting House and Barn, The Nook, Airton, Skipton, North Yorkshire, BD23 4AE
Tel: +44 1729 830623
Website: www.airtonbarn.org.uk
Email: airtonbarn@gmail.com
Overnight stays: £17 per person/night

Horton-in-Ribblesdale

The Golden Lion Hotel & Bunkhouse, Horton-in-Ribblesdale, Settle, North Yorkshire, BD24 0HB
Tel: +44 1729 860206
Website: www.goldenlionhotel.co.uk
Email: bookings@goldenlionhotel.co.uk
Bed & breakfast: Double or twin room £70 per night, full occupancy; single room £45 (per night, weekdays), £70 (per nights, Fri/Sat)

Bunk room: £12 per person/night (no bedding etc. is provided)
Packed lunches: £4.95; 3-course dinner approx. £16

Holme Farm Campsite, Horton-in-Ribblesdale, Settle, North Yorkshire, BD24 0HB
Tel: +44 1756 860281
Website: www.horton-in-ribblesdale.com/holme-farm-campsite.shtml
Camping: £4 for tent, £3 per person/night

3 Peaks Bunkroom, Horton-in-Ribblesdale, Settle, North Yorkshire, BD24 0HB
Tel: +44 1729 860380/+44 7870849419
Website: www.3peaksbunkroom.co.uk
Email: bookings@3peaksbunkroom.co.uk
Individual beds: £15 per person/night

Hawes

Bainbridge Ings Caravan & Camp Site, Hawes, North Yorkshire, DL8 3NU
Tel: +44 1969 667354
Website: www.bainbridge-ings.co.uk
Email: janet@bainbridge-ings.co.uk
Camping: £6 per person/night (hikers can book in advance)

Blackburn Farm & Trout Fishery, Gayle, Hawes, North Yorkshire, DL8 3NX
Tel: +44 1969 667524
Website: www.blackburnfarmhawes.com
Email: blackburnfarm@outlook.com
Camping: £7 per person/night

Hardraw Old School Bunkhouse, Hardraw, Hawes, North Yorkshire, DL8 3LZ
Tel: +44 1969 666034/+44 7546894317
Website: www.hardrawoldschoolbunkhouse.co.uk
Email: enquiries@hardrawschoolhouse.co.uk
Individual beds: £15 per person/night

Old Hall Cottage Campsite, Hardraw, Hawes, North Yorkshire, DL8 3LZ
Tel: +44 1969 667691
Website: www.oldhallcottagecampsite.co.uk
Bookings by telephone only. Please do NOT make contact via e-mail.
Camping: £6 per person/night

The Green Dragon Inn & Bunkhouse, Hardraw, Hawes, North Yorkshire, DL8 3LZ
Tel: +44 1969 667392
Website: www.greendragonhardraw.com/home.html
Email: stay@greendragonhardraw.com
Inn lodging: A variety of ensuite rooms priced from £35 per person/night (price does not include breakfast).
Bunkhouse beds: £15 per person/night

YHA Hawes, Lancaster Terrace, Hawes, North Yorkshire, DL8 3LQ
Tel: +44 845 371 9120
Website: www.yha.org.uk/hostel/hawes
Email: hawes@yha.org.uk

Beds in shared single sex rooms, adults: £20.50 - £28; private room sleeps ups to 2 people: £49-£55

Keld

Keld Bunkbarn & Campsite, Park House, Keld, North Yorkshire, DL11 6DZ
TeL: +44 1748 886549 (Bunkbarn enquiries/bookings), +44 1748 886159 (Campsite enquiries/bookings)
Website: www.keldbunkbarnandyurts.com
Email: info@keldbunkbarn.com/ For camping: info@swaldaleyurts.com
Camping: £8 per person/night
Bunkhouse beds: £21 per person/night

Rukin's Park Lodge Campsite, Keld, Richmond, North Yorkshire, DL11 6LJ
Tel: +44 1748 886274
Website: www.rukins-keld.co.uk
Email: rukins@btinternet.com (Enquiries only. No bookings are taken for this site.)
Camping: £5 per person/night

Tan Hill

Tan Hill Inn, Reeth, Richmond, Swaledale, Richmond, North Yorkshire, DL11 6ED
Tel: +44 1833 628 246
Website: www.tanhillinn.com
Email: info@tanhillinn.com
Camping: £5 per person/night

Baldersdale

Blackton Grange Farmhouse, Blackton, Baldersdale, County Durham, DL12 9UP
Tel: +44 1833 650629
Website: www.blacktongrangefarmhouse.com
10 bedrooms that sleep up to 40 people. Also camping area in adjoining field. Contact directly to discuss requirements/prices.

Middleton-in-Teesdale

Highside Farm, Bow bank, Middleton in Teesdale, Co Durham, DL12 0NT
Tel: +44 1833 640135
Website: www.highsidefarm.co.uk
Email: richard@highsidefarm.co.uk
Camping: £9 per person/night

Leekworth Caravan & Camping Park, Leekworth Lane, Middleton-in-Teesdale, Co Durham, DL12 0TL
Tel: +44 1833 640 582
Website: www.caravancampingteesdale.co.uk
Email: leekworthcaravanpark@live.co.uk
Tent Pitch (NO Electric) 2 adults, Sunday to Thursday £16.50; Friday & Saturday £17.50, Backpackers £8.50

The Kingsway Centre & Teesdale Camping Pod, Alston Road, Middleton-in-Teesdale, County Durham, DL12 0UU
Tel: +44 1833 640881/+44 7531 610986
Website: www.kingswaycentre.co.uk / www.teesdalecampingpod.net
Email: adam@kingswaycentre.co.uk
Camping pod: £25 per night for two people; £15 per night for one person
Bunkbed accommodation: £16 per person/night

Langdon Beck

East Underhurth Farm, Forest-in-Teesdale, County Durham, DL12 0HB
Tel: + 44 1833 622062
Email: eastunderhurthfarm@hotmail.co.uk
B&B: Rooms from £25 per person/night
Camping: £5 per person/ night

YHA Langdon Beck, Forest-in-Teesdale, Barnard Castle, County Durham, DL12 0XN
Tel: +44 845 371 9027
Website: www.yha.org.uk/hostel/langdon-beck
Email: langdonbeck@yha.org.uk
Beds in shared single sex rooms, adults: £15; private room sleeps ups to 2 people: £39

Dufton

Brow Farm Bed & Breakfast & Self Catering Barns, Dufton, Appleby, Cumbria, CA16 6DF
Tel: +44 17683 52865/+44 7891296813
Website: www.browfarm.com
Email: stay@browfarm.com
B&B: Rooms from £35 per person/night

Grandie Caravan Park, R&M Appleby Ltd, Old Dufton Hall Farmhouse, Dufton, Appleby, Cumbria, CA16 6DD
Tel: +44 17683 53582/ Julie: +44 7825148885/ Mike: +44 7736394509
Website: www.duftoncaravanpark.co.uk
Email: randm@dufton.org.uk
Camping: Low season £7; high season £8 per person/night including electric

YHA Dufton, Dufton, Appleby, Cumbria, CA16 6DB
Tel: +44 845 371 9734
Website: www.yha.org.uk/hostel/dufton
Email: dufton@yha.org.uk
Beds in shared single sex rooms, adults: £15; private room, sleeps ups to 2 people: £39

Garrigill

Garrigill Village Hall, Garrigill, Alston, Cumbria, CA9 3DS
Tel: + 44 1434 647516
Website: www.the-village-hall.webnode.com
Email: bookings@garrigillvh.org.uk
Bunkhouse: £12 per person/night
Camping: £5 per person/night

Alston

Haggs Bank Bunkhouse & Camping, Nentsberry, Alston, Cumbria, CA9 3LH
Tel: +44 1434 382486/+44 7919 092403
Website: www.haggsbank.com
Email: info@haggsbank.com
Bunkhouse: £20 per person/night
Camping: £8 per person/night

Tyne Willows Caravan Site, Station Road, Alston, Cumbria, CA9 3HZ
Tel: +44 1434 382515 (Bookings by telephone only.)
Camping: £5 per person/night

YHA Alston, The Firs, Alston, Cumbria, CA9 3RW
Tel: +44 1434 381509
Website: www.yha.org.uk/hostel/alston
Email: alston@yha.org.uk
Beds in shared single sex rooms, adults: £21.50 - £25; private room sleeps up to 2 people: £44

Greenhead

Holmhead Guest House & Camping Barn, Greenhead, Northumberland, CA8 7HY
Tel: + 44 16977 47402
Website: www.bandb-hadrianswall.co.uk
Email: holmhead@forestbarn.com
Camping barn: £13.50 per person/night or £60 for exclusive use of Barn 1
Camping: £5 per person/night

Hadrians Wall Camping & Caravan Site, Melkridge Tilery, Nr Haltwhistle, Northumberland, NE49 9PG
Tel: +44 1434 320495
Website: www.hadrianswallcampsite.co.uk
Email: info@hadrianswallcampsite.co.uk
Bunk barn: £15 per person/night
Camping: £10 off-peak/£13 peak season, per person/night

The Greenhead Hotel & Hostel, Greenhead, Brampton, Carlisle, Cumbria, CA8 7HB
Tel: +44 1697 747411
Website: www.greenheadhotelandhostel.co.uk
Email: enquiries@greenheadhotelandhostel.co.uk
B&B: All rooms are available at £80 per night for double or twin/£50 for single occupancy (including breakfast).
Hostel: Beds in the dormitory accommodation £15 per person/night.

Caw Gap

Winshields Farm Camp Site, Winshields Farm, Military Road, Bardon Mill, Hexham, Northumberland, NE47 7AN
Tel: +44 1434 344243
Website: www.winshields.co.uk
Email: winshields-bardonmill@btconnect.com

Bunkhouse: £12 per person/night
Camping: £9 per person/night

Once Brewed

Gibbs Hill Farm, Once Brewed, Bardon Mill, Northumberland, NE47 7AP
Tel: +44 1434 344030
Website: www.gibbshillfarm.co.uk
Email: val@gibbshillfarm.co.uk
Bunkhouse hostel: £18 per person/night

Stonehaugh

Stonehaugh Campsite, The Old Farmhouse, Stonehaugh Shields, Hexham, Northumberland, NE48 3BU
Tel: +44 1434 230798
Website: www.stonehaughcampsite.com
Email: enquiries@stonehaughcampsite.com
Camping: £9 per person/night

Bellingham

Bellingham Camping and Caravanning Club Site, Brown Rigg, Bellingham, Northumberland, NE48 2JY
Tel: +44 1434 220175
Web: www.campingandcaravanningclub.co.uk/campsites/uk/northumberland/hexham/bellingham
Email: bellingham.site@campingandcaravanningclub.co.uk
Camping: From £7 to £11.80 per person/night

Demesne Farm Campsite & Bunkhouse, Bellingham, Hexham, Northumberland, NE48 2BS
Tel: +44 1434 220258
Website: www.demesnefarmcampsite.co.uk
Email: stay@demesnefarmcampsite.co.uk
Bunkhouse: £20 per person/night
Camping: £7 per person/night

YHA Bellingham Bunkhouse, Hexham, Northumberland, NE48 2BS
Tel: +44 1434 220258
Website: www.yha.org.uk/hostel/bellingham-bunkhouse
Email: bellingham@yha.org.uk
Beds in shared single sex rooms only, adults: £20

Byrness

Border Forest Caravan Park, Cottonshopeburnfoot, Near Otterburn, Northumberland, NE19 1TF
Tel: +44 1830 520259
Website: www.borderforest.com
Email: info@borderforest.com
Camping Pod: from £35 per night for 2 adults, includes electrics
Camping: £8 per person/night (£9 for July & August)

Forest View Inn, 6-8 Otterburn Green, Byrness Village, Northumberland, NE19 1TS
Tel: +44 1830 520425/+44 7928376677
Website: www.forestviewbyrness.co.uk
Email: joycetaylor1703@hotmail.co.uk
Rooms: Single, Twin or Triple, Dinner, B & B £49.50 per person/night
Camping and use of lounge, drying room and shower block free when ordering a 3 course evening meal. Please ring to reserve as pitches are limited.
*2 night package with bus ride to Cheviot halfway point, to split the Cheviot section. Ring for details.

Option for the Cheviots

The Farmhouse at Yetholm Mill, Main St, Kirk Yetholm, Kelso, Roxburghshire, TD5 8PE
Tel: +44 1573 420505 (all bookings & enquiries by phone)
Website: www.thefarmhouseatkirkyetholm.com
Pennine Way Package includes: 2 nights' accommodation (Bed & Breakfast) in twin, double, or king room. Packed lunch on final day. Transport to and from Cocklawfoot.
£120 - £130 single occupancy; £195 - £215 double occupancy.

Kirk Yetholm

Kirk Yetholm Friends of Nature House, Friends of Nature House, Waukford, Kirk Yetholm, Roxburghshire, TD5 8PG
Tel: +44 1573 420639
Website: www.independenthostels.co.uk/members/kirkyetholmfriendsofnaturehouse
Email: kirkyetholm@thefriendsofnature.org.uk
Beds in shared single sex rooms, adults: £18; private room sleeps ups to 2 people: £40

Border Hotel, The Green, Kirk Yetholm, Kelso, Roxburghshire, TD5 8PQ
Tel: +44 1573 420237
Website: www.theborderhotel.com
Email: theborderhotel@gmail.com
Double rooms from £40 per person/night. Single occupancy £50 - £60. Price includes full Scottish breakfast.

Note: Some bed and breakfast options have also been listed if this is the only accommodation available.

D. Distance Chart

Below is a basic overview of approximate distances between towns and villages on the Pennine Way. The figures given are rounded to the nearest mile and any deviations from official distances are due to slight route variations over the course of the trail. They exclude any diversions or alternate routes, and do not take account of extra distances off the trail to and from accommodation. The stages here add up to 262 miles, as simplified and explained in Section 3a *Trails & Navigation*.

From / To	Distances (miles)
Kirk Yetholm	262 247 246 235 224 220 219 208 203 196 191 187 185 170 156 144 140 131 128 117 109 98 82 78 58 55 47 40 25 0
Byrness	237 222 221 210 199 195 194 183 178 171 166 162 160 145 131 119 115 106 103 92 84 73 57 53 33 30 22 15 0 Kirk Yetholm
Bellingham	222 207 206 195 184 180 179 168 163 156 151 147 145 130 116 104 100 91 88 77 69 58 42 38 18 15 7 0 Byrness
Stonehaugh	215 200 199 188 177 173 172 161 156 149 144 140 138 123 109 97 93 84 81 70 62 51 35 31 11 8 0 Bellingham
Once Brewed	207 192 191 180 169 165 164 153 148 141 136 132 130 115 101 89 85 76 73 62 54 43 27 23 3 0 Stonehaugh
Haltwhistle	204 189 188 177 166 162 161 150 145 138 133 129 127 112 98 86 82 73 70 59 51 40 24 20 0 Once Brewed
Greenhead	201 186 185 174 163 159 158 147 142 135 130 126 124 109 95 83 79 70 67 56 48 37 21 17 0 Haltwhistle
Alston	184 169 168 157 146 142 141 130 125 118 113 109 107 92 78 66 62 53 50 39 31 20 4 0 Greenhead
Garrigill	180 165 164 153 142 138 137 126 121 114 109 105 103 88 74 62 58 49 46 35 27 16 0 Alston
Dufton	164 149 148 137 126 122 121 110 105 98 93 89 87 72 58 46 42 33 30 19 11 0 Garrigill
Langdon Beck	153 138 137 126 115 111 110 99 94 87 82 78 76 61 47 35 31 22 19 8 0 Dufton
Middleton-in-Teesdale	145 130 129 118 107 103 102 91 86 79 74 70 68 53 39 27 23 14 11 0 Langdon Beck
Baldersdale	134 119 118 107 96 92 91 80 75 68 63 59 57 42 28 16 12 3 0 Middleton in Teesdale
Bowes / A66	131 116 115 104 93 89 88 77 72 65 60 56 54 39 25 13 9 0 Baldersdale
Tan Hill	122 107 106 95 84 80 79 68 63 56 51 47 45 30 16 4 0 Bowes / A66
Keld	118 103 102 91 80 76 75 64 59 52 47 43 41 26 12 0 Tan Hill
Hawes	106 91 90 79 68 64 63 52 47 40 35 31 29 14 0 Keld
Horton-in-Ribblesdale	92 77 76 65 54 50 49 38 33 26 21 17 15 0 Hawes
Malham	77 62 61 50 39 35 34 23 18 11 6 2 0 Horton in Ribblesdale
Airton	75 60 59 48 37 33 32 21 16 9 4 0 Malham
Gargrave	71 56 55 44 33 29 28 17 12 5 0 Airton
Thornton-in-Craven	66 51 50 39 28 24 23 12 7 0 Gargrave
Cowling	59 44 43 32 21 17 16 5 0 Thornton-in-Craven
Ponden	54 39 38 27 16 12 11 0 Cowling
Colden	43 28 27 16 5 1 0 Ponden
Hebden Bridge	42 27 26 15 4 0 Colden
Mankinholes	38 23 22 11 0 Hebden Bridge
Standedge / A62	27 12 11 0 Mankinholes
Crowden	16 1 0 Standedge / A62
Torside	15 0 Crowden
Edale	0 Torside

Distance Chart (miles)

Appendices 179

E. Elevation Profiles

The elevation profiles are based on GPS data recorded during the authors' walk. Deviations from the official distances are due to slight route variations over the course of the trail. For instance, the authors did not take the Bowes loop or the Cheviot summit option.

In all the profiles, the vertical axis represents the elevation (in metres and feet) and the horizontal axis represents the distance (in miles). Note the horizontal distance is not to scale! Each major town/village is indicated on the profiles so you can immediately see what elevation gain/loss you will encounter for each of your hiking days.

You can also use the profiles to gauge how far you wish to hike during the day with respect to the effort required between a particular day's start and end points. E.g. if the terrain is flatter, you may wish to extend your day and hike further so as to make the next day easier and/or shorter.

Appendices 181

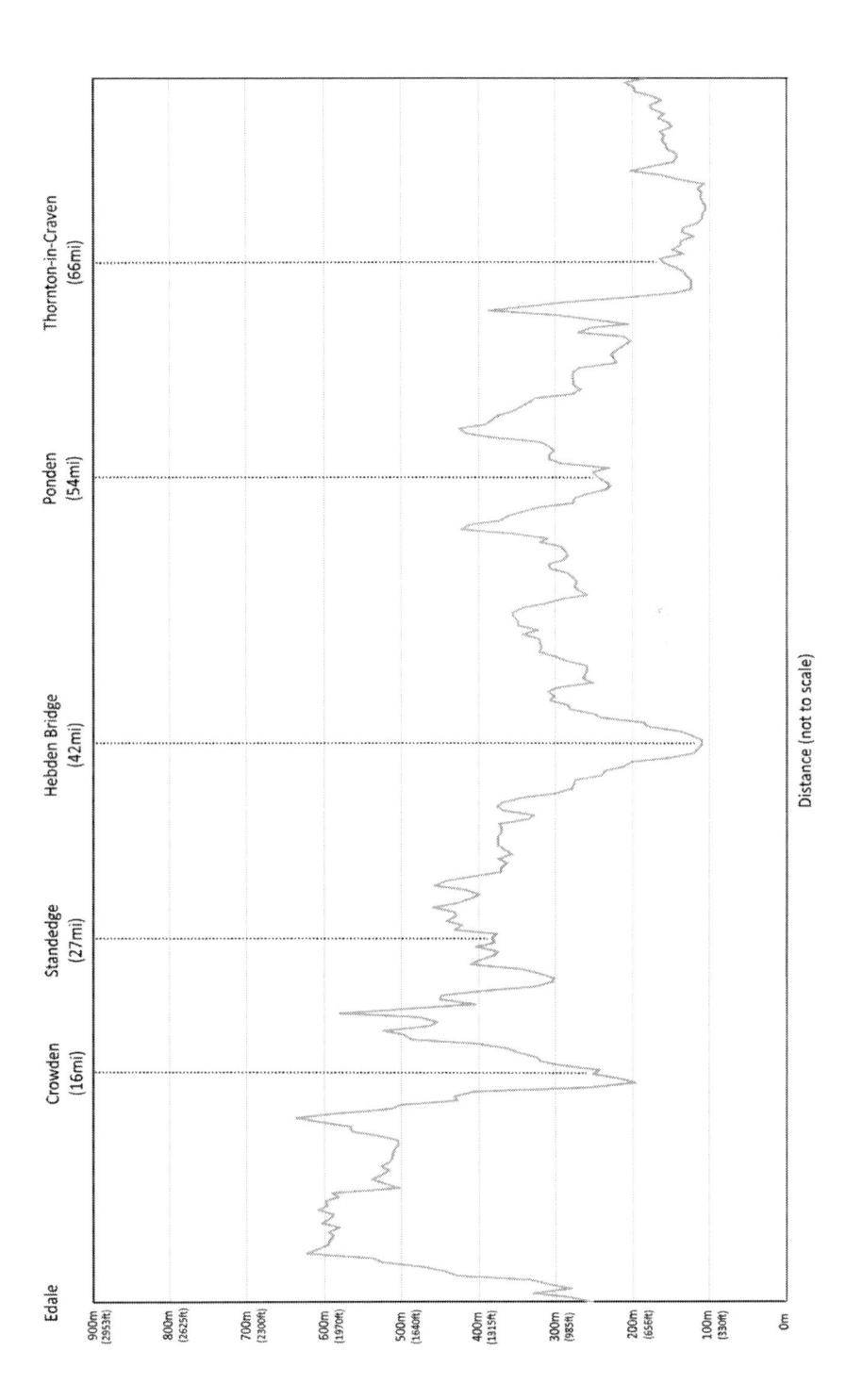

182 Appendices

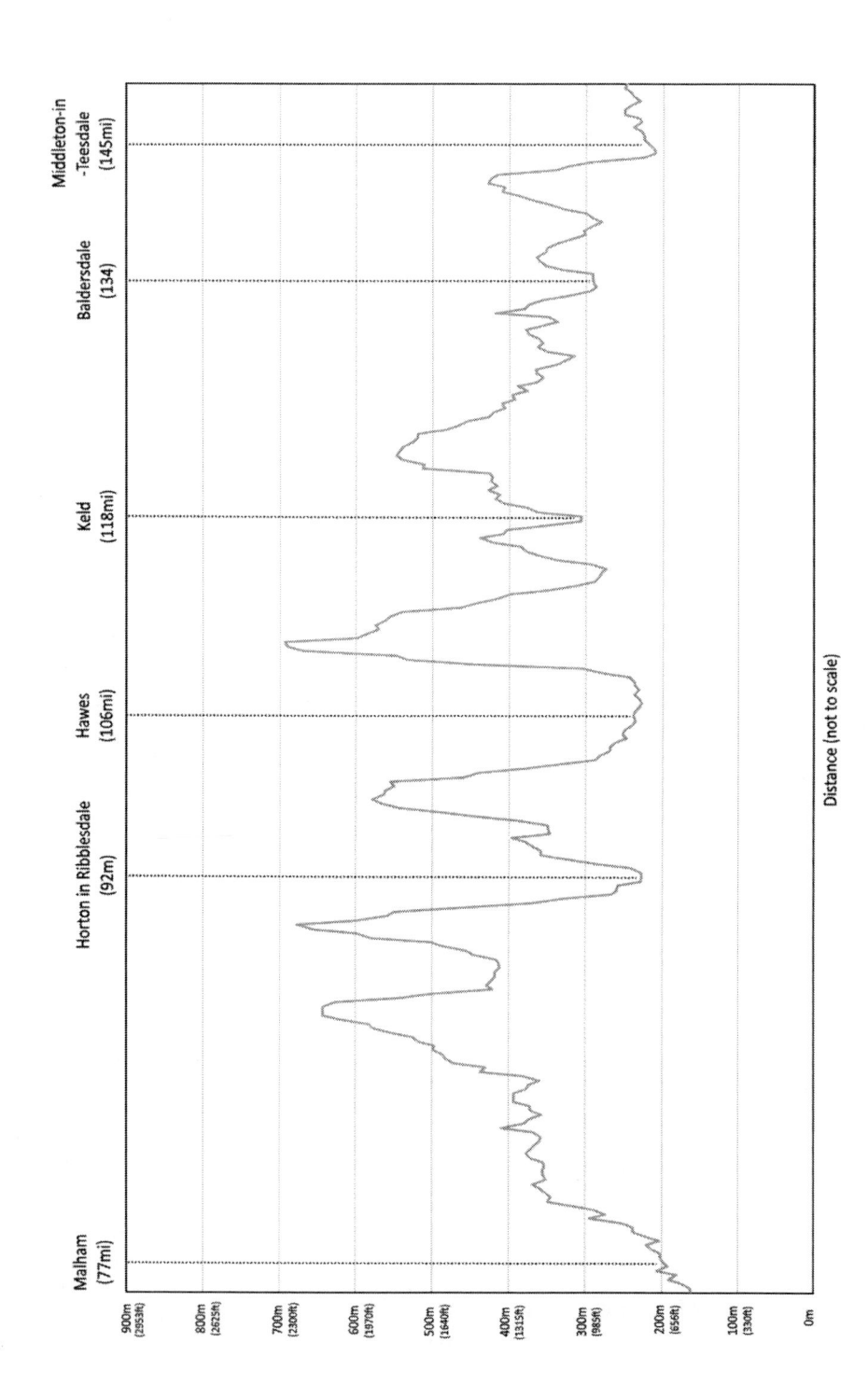

Appendices   183

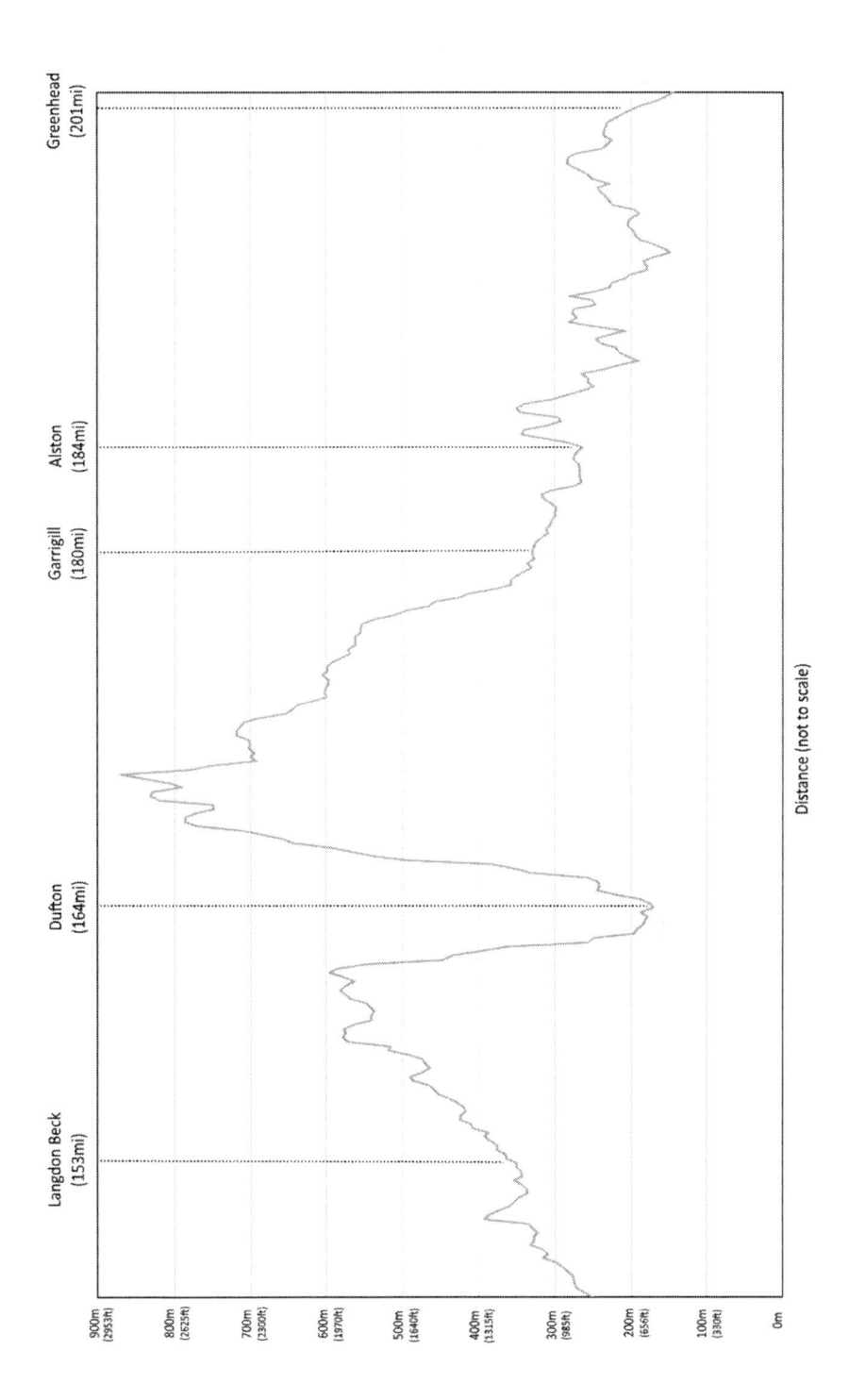

184　*Appendices*

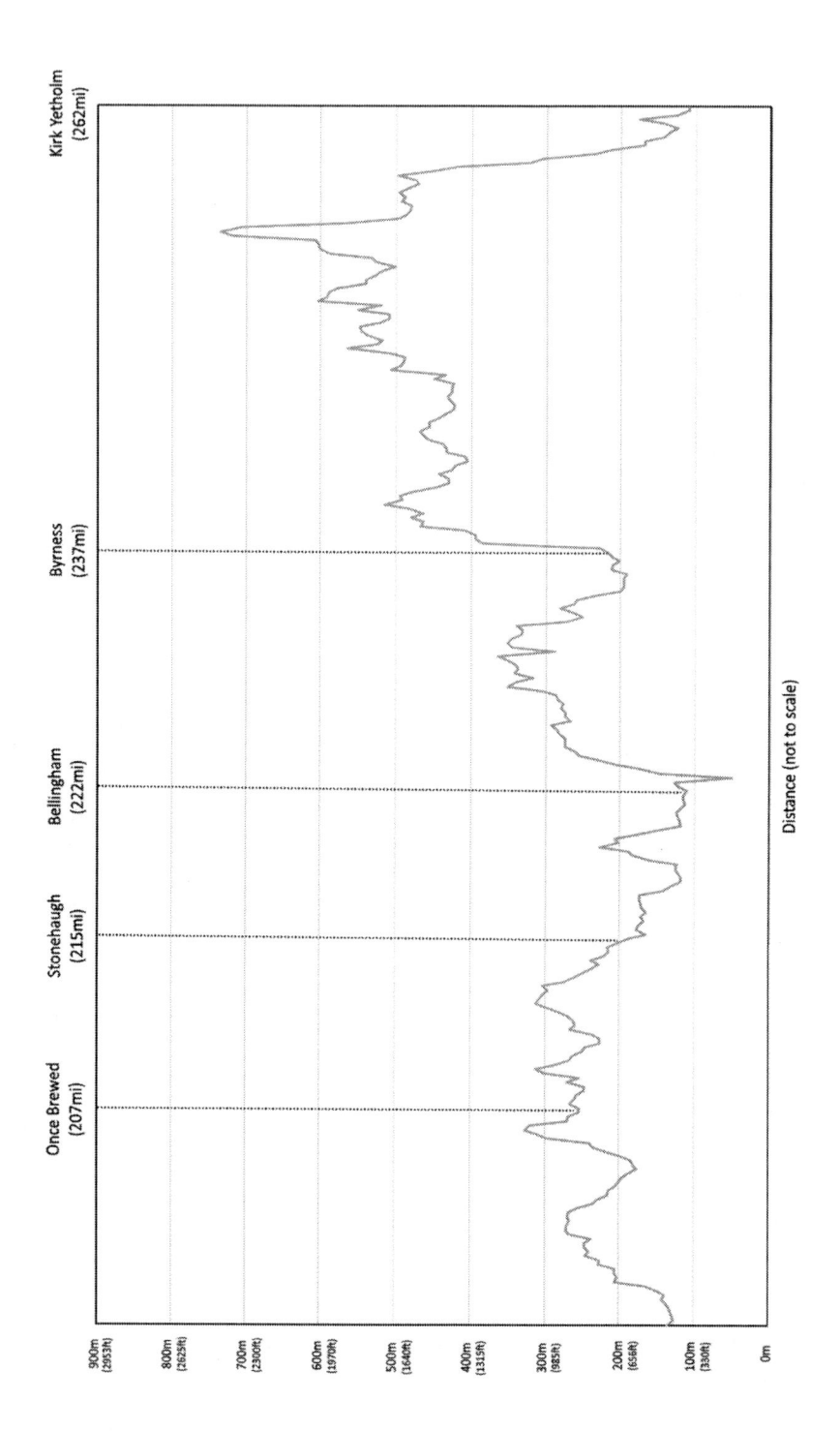

F. Links & References

Pennine Way Planner

Plan your personalised visit to the trail with maps, a distance calculator, trail information and latest news.

-- http://www.nationaltrail.co.uk/pennine-way/plan

Pennine Way Accommodation

A useful online Pennine Way accommodation guide is also available on the **National Trails** website. The guide is interactive and can show you which type of lodging is available at different places on a route map. You can specifically click to show one type of accommodation only e.g. all campsites along the route. All listed accommodation has contact details and pricing.

-- http://www.nationaltrail.co.uk/pennine-way/plan

Pennine Way Logistical Services

If you are interested in using a logistical service company to carry baggage, transport you from start/end points, or book accommodation for your Pennine Way trip, the following companies have good reputations for service.

-- http://www.sherpavan.com (Service runs daily south to north from Malham to Kirk Yeltholm.)

-- http://www.brigantesenglishwalks.com/pennine-way/baggage-transfer/

Harvey Maps

Take a look at this website when deciding what maps you will purchase for your Pennine Way walk.

-- http://www.harveymaps.co.uk/index.html

National Rail Enquiries, UK

The gateway to Britain's National Rail Network. A portal into UK rail travel including train company information and promotions, train schedules, fare enquiries, ticket bookings, and travel alerts.

-- http://www.nationalrail.co.uk

Recreational Equipment, Inc. (REI)

Wide-ranging outdoor advice & products:

-- *http://www.rei.com/learn/expert-advice.html*

The Pennine Way Association

Although the Association closed as of January 2016, the website remains a good source of information regarding the history of the Pennine Way. In particular, there is an accommodation guide that can be downloaded for free, news and route updates, as well as useful links to support you in your planning.

-- *http://penninewayassociation.co.uk/*

Tourist Information UK

Useful guides for tourists visiting the UK from abroad, packed with information and advice on accommodation, travel and weather. Also lots of useful information about the UK's favourite tourist attractions including pictures and photos, admission times, opening dates, ticket prices, location maps, and contact information. (Particularly useful if you intend on visiting points of interest or doing any side trips.)

-- *http://www.tourist-information-uk.com/guides/tourist-information-advice/uk-weather/*

Travel Line

Another good website to help you plan your journey. It is a partnership of transport companies, local authorities and passenger groups that have come together to provide routes and times for all travel in Great Britain by bus, rail, coach and ferry.

-- *http://www.traveline.info/*

UK Met Office

For the latest in-depth and up-to-date weather forecasts for the UK.

-- *http://www.metoffice.gov.uk/public/weather/forecast*

And, of course, visit:

www.PlanAndGoHiking.com

for more information, pictures, and posts.

We look forward to and appreciate your feedback!

G. List of Abbreviations

AONB	Areas of Outstanding Natural Beauty
ATM	Automated Teller Machine/Cash Dispenser
B&B	Bed & Breakfast
E2	European Long Distance Path – Route 2
ETD	Estimate of Trail Days
GPS	Global Positioning System
LED	Light Emitting Diode
MoD	Ministry of Defence
OS	Ordnance Survey (Britain's Mapping Agency)
£	British Pound (currency code: GBP)
p	Penny/Pence (currency code: GBP)
PO	Post Office
PW	Pennine Way
RAF	The Royal Air Force (UK's aerial warfare force)
LSC	Logistical Service Company
UK	United Kingdom
UNESCO	United Nations Educational, Scientific and Cultural Organization
YHA	Youth Hostels Association (England & Wales)

About the Authors

Wayne and Danielle, both born in England during the 1970s, have been a couple for 18 years. Their passion for the great outdoors was ignited during their first career break in 2010, where they bought a pair of walking boots for the first time and hiked in various parts of South East Asia, China, New Zealand, and the USA.

Since then, they have completed several thru-hikes around the world, including the 'W' trek in Torres del Paine, Chile, Colca Canyon in Peru, the Coast to Coast path across England, the John Muir Trail in the USA, the West Highland Way in Scotland, and the GR20 across Corsica, which they have documented on their 'hiking, travel, and adventure' blog *www.treksnappy.com*.

As Danielle puts pen to paper writing about their experiences on the trail, Wayne, being the keen photographer of the two, likes to capture the heart and soul of a place on camera, showing the wonders of nature through his images and time lapse sequences.

While they would love nothing more than to hike full time, currently, Wayne and Danielle are living and working in England, as a means of saving and preparing for their next outdoor adventure!

Special Thanks

We would like to thank our parents, without whom none of our hiking adventures would be possible. Not only have they put a roof over our heads, stored our most treasured possessions, and become foster parents to our two very spoilt cats; but they have also been instrumental to us achieving our goal of completing this journey by becoming our most loyal followers and dedicated 'Support Team'.

Words cannot express how grateful we are.

Disclaimer

The information provided in this book is accurate to the best of authors' and publisher's knowledge. However, there is no aspiration, guarantee, or claim to the correctness, completeness, and validity of any information given. Readers should be aware that internet addresses, phone numbers, mailing addresses, as well as prices, services, etc. were believed to be accurate at time of publication, but are subject to change without notice.

References are provided for informational purposes only. Neither authors nor the publisher have control over the content of websites, books, or other third party sources listed in this book and, consequently, do not accept responsibility for any content referred to herein. The mention of companies, organizations, or authorities in this book does not imply endorsement by authors or publisher, and vice versa.

This book is not a medical guidebook. The information and advice provided herein are merely intended as reference and explicitly not as a substitute for professional medical advice. Consult a physician to discuss whether or not your health and fitness level are appropriate for the physical activities describe in this book; especially, if you are aware of any pre-existing conditions or issues.

All rights reserved. No part of this publication may be reproduced or transmitted in any form or by any means, electronically or mechanically, including photocopying, scanning, recording, or any other information storage and retrieval systems, without written permission of the publisher, except for brief quotations in reviews.

Copyright © 2016 by Danielle Fenton, Wayne Fenton, and sandiburg press

Printed in Great Britain
by Amazon